When the Pig goes to Market

All the best!

When the Pig goes to Market

How to Achieve Long-term Investing Success

DAVID CORK

WITH SUSAN LIGHTSTONE

Published in 1999 by Stoddart Publishing Co. Limited
34 Lesmill Road, Toronto, Canada M3B 2T6
180 Varick Street, 9th Floor, New York, New York 10014

For information about U.S. publication and distribution of Stoddart Books, contact
180 Varick Street, 9th Floor, New York, NY 10014

Distributed in Canada by:
General Distribution Services Ltd.
325 Humber College Boulevard, Toronto, Canada M9W 7C3
Tel. (416) 213-1919   Fax (416) 213-1917
Email customer.service@ccmailgw.genpub.com

03 02 01 00 99 1 2 3 4 5

Canadian Cataloguing in Publication Data

Cork, David
When the pig goes to market: how to achieve long-term investing success

Includes bibliographic references

ISBN 0-7737-6025-3

1. Finance, Personal — Canada. 2. Baby boom generation — Canada. I. Lightstone, Susan. II. Title.
HG179.C663 1999 332.024'00771 C98-933092-3

Cover Design: Bill Douglas @ The Bang
Design and typesetting: Kinetics Design & Illustration

Printed and bound in Canada

Stoddart Publishing gratefully acknowledges the Canada Council for the Arts and the Ontario Arts Council for their support of its publishing program.

To the four women who make my life
so very interesting and rewarding,
Peggy, Emily, Meagan, and Julia
— D.C.

To my constant friends — boomers, of course —
Margo Takeda and Bev Jensen
— S.L.

Contents

Acknowledgements

Writing a book is assumed to be a solitary sport. Yes, there *are* many long hours alone, spent thinking, reading, writing. But this book, like its predecessor, *The Pig and the Python*, has been a collaborative effort. In fact, one of the great pleasures of bringing this book to press has been the people with whom Susan Lightstone and I have had the pleasure of talking and working. The people who became involved — entwined, in many cases — in the process are smart, funny and incredibly generous with their time and thoughts. I hope that their good spirits shine through in a book that is, after all, about people.

My colleagues at ScotiaMcLeod — James Werry, James McPhedran and David Nicol, in particular — have provided solid support since I started out on my demographic odyssey. I am the first to admit that learning is a constant process, and I am privileged to have some stellar teachers, including Dr. David K. Foot and his colleagues at the Madison Avenue Demographics Group. Thank you also to Daniel Stoffman, Bill Sterling, Stephen Waite, Tim Griffin, Allan Shaw and Louise Yamada for sharing your ideas with me. To fellow authors David Chilton and Ranga Chand, thank you for your support and guidance along the way. Special thanks to Pierre Laframboise for his comments on the psychology of boomers and to Kamal Dhar who offered his profound insights into the difference between contentedness and happiness. Once again, Michael Smythe and David Crawford served as valuable sounding boards for my ideas. Thanks, gentlemen.

Many professionals provided us with information concerning their areas of expertise: John Pigott, Professor George Dix, Dr. Richard V. Hodder, Mark Jensen, Mark Alberdingk Thijm, Sandra Dunn, Karen Mazur, Laura Peck, Barry McLoughlin, Dr. Meridith Marks and Peter Bruneau. Thank you! Several literary friends found themselves roped into reading chapters as they appeared and responded with artful comments. My gratitude to Bill Kretzel, Janis Hass and Barbara Sibbald.

There are plenty of folks behind the scenes who make my work possible. Without the cheerful support of my co-workers Janette Andrews, Jason Brazeau and Shari Bean, it would have been impossible for me to write this book. Our team at Stoddart Publishing, Don Bastian, Shaun Oakey, Stephen Quick and Mary Giuliano, provided helpful insights throughout the writing process.

Susan and I would like to thank our families for their

support and patience. To our spouses Peggy and Lyon and our amazing children, Emily, Meagan, and Julia Cork, and Adrian and Nicola Lightstone — thank you.

Finally, heartfelt gratitude to the readers of *The Pig and the Python*. You surprised and thrilled us with your devotion to *The Pig*. Keep those cards and letters coming!

DAVID CORK
Ottawa

Introduction

This time it's different. That phrase – uttered in the context of the financial markets – is guaranteed to generate a smirk, followed by a patronizing nod of the head and the sarcastic response: "Now where have I heard *that* before?" The implication these naysayers wish to establish? Things just don't change.

So why did we choose this phrase to serve as the cornerstone of our book? Ask anyone around you, whether your spouse, your next-door neighbour or the guy sitting next to you on the bus: "Have you been affected by change recently?" I guarantee the answer will be "yes." People's lives are different now. Some of these people have been downsized from their jobs, or they're using computers in ways they never thought possible, or maybe they're less certain about the future than they thought they'd be at this point in life. Things *are* changing and the pace of change is accelerating, making the world a different place. And one of the critical agents of this change is the huge generation of middle-aged adults we call the baby boomers, the pig in the python of Canadian society.

Technology is changing our lives for the good and, sometimes, not so good. Globalization has introduced unparalleled opportunities for Canada and its citizens, but it's also created unsettling challenges around the world, particularly in the financial marketplace. We are living in interesting times and an aging population will continue to change the Canada we know. A very expensive generation to raise and educate, the boomers, older and wiser, are now paying dividends on the investment that Canada made in them.

Intuitively, middle-aged Canadians seem to sense the importance of the next 10 to 15 years in their financial lives, as they strive to plan and put their finances in order. Since the launch of our first book, *The Pig and the Python*, I have had the pleasure of travelling across Canada and talking to many of these people at my seminars about the impact of the boom on investing in Canada. With this book, *When the Pig Goes to Market*, I am trying to answer the many comments and questions that I have heard over the past three years. One of the notions that I hope to dispel here is the idea held by many busy boomers: If I can just get through this week, this month, this year, *then* I'll get around to organizing my financial affairs. Welcome to your life, folks. These are the busiest years that we will ever experience, between work, kids and aging parents, and unless you turn your mind now to embarking on the planning, saving and investing process, the opportunity could easily pass you by.

In this story about differences and the opportunities they present for a generation headed into their crucial retirement-planning years, we've married our theme with the recognition that change is a constant. One thing that never changes is that we will always face change. The trick lies in recognizing that fact and profiting from it.

Once again, our characters, Hazen and the gang, are back — older and, we hope, wiser. We've set the book in the summer and fall of 1998 — a span of time that is representative of any six-month period faced by an investor. Just as our lives have cycles, the market moves through cycles, some more pleasant than others. We hope this book will help investors look long-term, beyond this week, this month, this year, and recognize that, like life, it's worth sticking with the stock market for the long haul.

Invest well!

1

Just the Beginning

"What is so rare as a day in June?" These were the words roaming through my head as I stretched out in bed that Saturday morning in June. The sun was streaming through the window, I could hear the soft voices of the kids next door already playing outside. A lawn mower roared into action somewhere on the next block. How did the rest of that darn quotation go? It was one of my dad's favourites, usually uttered as he stood on our front stoop savouring a warm June day. I could see him — he'd be in his old gardening clothes, mug of coffee in hand. It had something to do with perfection. Where do words go when you want them? And then it came to me, right out of the blue: "Then, if ever, come perfect days."

What a good way to wake up — to warm memories and pleasant thoughts. I checked the clock; just after eight. Perfect! I looked over to Pieter, still asleep. He'd been putting in some long hours at work. Let him snooze, I decided. I rolled out of bed quietly, stuffed on my slippers and shrugged that plaid housecoat over my long flannel nightgown. I laughed silently at my outfit — why does Victoria's Secret bother sending a catalogue to this address? Pieter seemed to get more out of it than I did.

I peeked into the kids' rooms — both still asleep. Ah! This really was the start of a rare day. I'd pick up the paper, make a pot of coffee and enjoy an hour or two of solitude. Great!

But life doesn't always head where you think it will. Sometimes, it turns out better.

I opened the front door and began the search for the newspaper. Its exact location each morning was anybody's guess — sometimes we'd find it in the mailbox, other times under the front mat, occasionally stuck in the bushes. Today, it was halfway down the walk. I quickly surveyed the street — nobody around; nobody to see my lovely nightwear. Good. I stepped out, picked up the paper and was just turning back indoors when a familiar voice called out through the stillness.

"Meredith! Meredith DeMarco! I knew I'd find you out here about now. Can we talk?"

It was Hazen Armstrong, my neighbour across the street. Standing at his fence, he was already dressed for the day. How I envied Hazen's energy level. In his early sixties, he kept a schedule that would exhaust a person half his age. For the past 20 years, he's acted as a consultant, advising both private and corporate investors where and how to invest. Hazen is a demographics expert. He studies the numerical facts of human populations — how many teenagers we've got, how many senior citizens, that sort of thing.

Hazen is most interested in the baby boom, that demographic aberration that dropped well over nine million babies in Canada from 1947 to 1965. For several years now, he has taken his show on the road, speaking to large groups of investors about the influence of demographics, in particular the aging baby boom, on investment markets. "The Pig and the Python" is what he calls his presentation, a reference to that huge bulge of baby boomers sitting in the middle of the Canadian economy; smaller generations are on each end of the python. Hazen focuses on the changes that can be expected in the Canadian economy as the boomer generation ages and moves through our society. He's an astute observer of the digestion process, watching the pig travel along the length of the python. "Common sense," he would always say. "People affect things, and large groups of people affect things in a large way."

When we first met Hazen Armstrong, he was the neighbourhood mystery man — nobody knew what he did for a living. Not any more. Since our move into the neighbourhood two years ago, Hazen has become well known as Canada's dean of demographics. At first, seeing our neighbour on the TV news was a novelty, but now he's a regular talking head. He keeps telling us that he's not one bit surprised by his instant acclaim. "If people would only listen to what the boom is telling them," he'd say. "Of course they're interested in investing now. They're the right age for it — between 33 and 51.

Their big-spending years are behind them, and now they're starting to save for retirement. The cavalry has ridden in — now nearly 10 million strong, when you count both those born in Canada and those born elsewhere."

Not only is Hazen famous, he's been great to us. When Pieter and I arrived in the Glebe, we were somewhat shell-shocked. Pieter's business — he's a software designer who owns a company with two partners — had hit some rough times. Our income had fallen dramatically and we were forced to sell our house in the suburbs. I wasn't working outside the home at that point, having committed myself to staying home with our two kids until they were both in school full time. So when Pieter's income hit the skids, that was it — we were mortgaged to the hilt and had to move or risk bankruptcy. It was a tough time for both of us. Then we met Hazen.

Hazen didn't turn our lives around. We did that ourselves. But he did a lot to get us back on track. Until we met Hazen, we'd been preoccupied with spending money. Hazen explained why it was now important for us to begin saving. Then he gave us some good pointers on where to put that money we'd saved.

Hazen also introduced me to Ruth Schneider, a sociology professor at the University of Ottawa and very close friend of his; not only do they share a passion for the study of demographics but they also have a son together. Hazen and Ruth never married, never even lived together, although they've spent a lot of time together raising their son — family vacations and other fun stuff. Hazen jokes that he and Ruth invented the alternative lifestyle. Their family relationship had changed as their son, Dylan, grew up. Now in his early twenties, Dylan has been studying for the past few years in the U.S. I knew both Hazen and Ruth missed the family time spent skiing, sailing and just hanging out.

Ruth hired me to assist with a study she was conducting on how the baby boom's stage of life affects society's view of itself. I just finished a two-year contract with Ruth and now I was looking for another research contract. Hazen has even given Pieter some helpful pointers for his business.

Hazen opened his gate and crossed the street. I strolled to the end of our walkway.

"I'll only take a couple minutes of your time," he said. "It looks as if you haven't had your first coffee of the day yet."

"Do I look that bad?" I smiled, curtsying in my housecoat.

"I didn't mean it like that, Meredith. I just meant to say . . ." Hazen sputtered.

This was good. I hadn't seen Hazen lost for words — ever. He seemed to have an answer for everything, always a statistic to prove a point or the perfect quote from an eminent source.

"It's okay, Hazen. I'm just kidding you. I figure we've known one another long enough to joke about my fashion statements. So, what do you want to talk about that can't wait until I'm dressed?"

"Work," he stated emphatically. "A research position, actually. I know you've finished your contract with Ruth. Now how would you like to work with me for a few months?"

Life is strange, isn't it? It was a lovely June morning. The lawn mower was still growling away around the corner. I could hear the kids next door, still playing in their sandbox. I was standing in my nightclothes, the fat Saturday *Citizen* weighing me down. I had awakened unemployed and now Hazen Armstrong was offering me a job. Sometimes, things turn out okay — if you let them!

"Hazen, that sounds very interesting. What do you need done?" Now that I'd had a moment to think about this, I was surprised by Hazen's offer. I was certain he did most of his own research, preparing his presentations on his own.

"I've been approached by a large financial institution wanting me to tour and speak to audiences who've already heard my speech — they expect more than the basics. In fact, the company has sent me a list of issues they want included. They're particularly concerned that the market is poised to correct. You recall that term, I'm sure," Hazen said with a slight chuckle.

Hazen was well aware of my naturally cautious disposition and my concerns about the market. We'd talked many times about the risks and rewards of the stock market, with Hazen working towards allaying my fears about losing hard-earned investments to the vagaries of the stock market.

"Right," I answered. "A correction occurs when the market drops by 10 percent from a recent high. How could I forget? It's what I dread. But it's a market crash that really frightens me — when the market plummets 20 percent or more in the space of a couple of days. Like back in October 1987."

"Ah, yes. I think we'll include a special reassuring heading for you nervous types. How does 'Lions, Tigers and Bears: What You Really Need to Know about Crashes and Corrections' sound?"

I smiled. "I'm sure I'd learn a thing or two. What other information do they want?"

"They've made some very good suggestions," said Hazen. "They're interested in the effects of global demographics on the North American economy. The populations of the Third World countries are rising faster than those of countries like Canada. Look at Turkey. They've already got a population of more than 60 million and a birth rate nearly double ours. Think about it. The population of the industrialized countries is going to shrink in relation to the populations of countries like Turkey. That's going to have a big impact on our economy."

"I guess it means our companies will be forced to go global," I suggested.

Hazen nodded. "If they want to keep growing over the long term, it probably does. But there's more. Immigration, for example. We tend to focus on the number of babies born in Canada. But our population also grows through immigration. On a typical day, we'll see an average of 1,000 babies born and approximately 600 immigrants arrive from foreign shores."

"That's incredible. I knew that Canada was a country of immigrants — look at my own family. We came from all over the world. But I had no idea the effect of immigration was still that profound."

"There's more. The list includes at least 10 topics they want me to address. It seems that people are starting to pay attention to this common-sense demographics information. But if I'm going to have this presentation ready by autumn, I've got to get cracking on it. And I'm definitely going to need some help."

"Hazen, I'm really interested in this project, but let me run in and pull on some clothes. Meet you on your porch in 10 minutes — I'll bring the java." I was becoming a bit self-conscious about conducting a business meeting in the middle of the street — in my pyjamas.

When I reappeared on our doorstep, I was ready for the day and carrying a tray loaded with coffee paraphernalia. I could see Hazen on his porch, buried in the morning newspaper.

"Hazen, I need some help," I shouted, motioning to his latched gate.

"Meredith, here's a coincidence," said Hazen, helping me through the gate. "Here, let me take the tray and you look at this article in today's paper."

I glanced at the headline: "The Savings Rate — A Statistical Whodunit."

"This is one of the topics the financial institution wants me to talk about," he said.

"Why? What's so important about our savings rate?" I asked. We arranged ourselves on Hazen's porch. Finally, I had my cup of coffee and I sat back, waiting to hear Hazen's response.

"In the 1990s, our savings rate — subtract spending from income and you get savings — has fallen. In 1995, it stood at 6.9 percent. By 1997, it had dipped under

2 percent. Evidently, plenty of people are arguing that, with rates like that, boomers aren't going to be ready for retirement."

"So, will they be prepared?" I asked.

"Good question. You tell me. That's just one of the questions I want you to work on over the next few months," he replied. "I want to talk about whether boomers can turn their minds and wallets to saving for their retirements. That glut of savings is going to have a huge and positive influence on Canada's financial markets."

"Right," I answered. "That's what you call the 'indirect' effect of the boomers on markets. They're bound to push markets upwards because of where they are in their lives — preparing and saving for retirement."

Hazen said, "But I also want to tell my audiences which industries and companies are poised to profit from the boom and which are on the skids because they haven't kept up with that pig in the python."

"The other half of the boomer equation," I shot back. "That's what you call the 'direct' effect of boomers on the stock market — when boomers influence the success of a company, causing the price of its stock to rise or fall."

"Exactly. I want to provide some colourful examples of companies that are doing the right thing and paying close attention to demographics. But I also want some stories of businesses that didn't watch the boom," he answered.

I laughed. "Well, I've got a really colourful story for you. I read about this company when I was doing my research for Ruth. Have you heard of Binney & Smith?"

"I can't say that I have," Hazen said slowly.

"Binney & Smith makes Crayola crayons — I told you

this was a colourful story," I said. "Crayons are a big hit with little kids. Three-to-seven-year-olds love 'em. Let me tell you, I've bought dozens of boxes of crayons over the years. The company took a look at the demographic statistics and saw that this market wasn't about to grow very much over the next few years. Not a great time for the crayon business. So they decided to broaden their focus to include kids aged eight to twelve."

"Smart move," Hazen acknowledged. "Those children form part of the echo generation, the children of the boom. Marketers refer to them as the 'tween' market — no longer little kids but not quite teenagers. Because there are so many boomers, their tweens form a mini-boom unto themselves, numbering almost 2.5 million. And they pack a punch in the marketplace. It's estimated that they directly control $1.4 billion worth of spending power. But that's only the tip of the iceberg. Think of the influence they have over their boomer parents, suggesting what restaurants to frequent, what movies to rent, what foods to buy. So what did Binney & Smith do?"

"They introduced a line called Crayola IQ — really cool coloured pencils, markers and other products that an older child wouldn't mind taking to school. Let's face it — an 11-year-old isn't going to head off to Grade 5 with a box of Crayola crayons in her backpack. Plus, the company aimed their marketing at the kids themselves rather than at their parents. Another smart move. Like you were saying, tweens have plenty of disposable income. And they definitely have their own taste and they want to do their own shopping. Anything I think is great, my kids deem decidedly uncool. Anyway, Binney & Smith's sales jumped by something like 50 percent last year." I was proud of my ability to remember all this so early on a Saturday morning.

"That's precisely the sort of information I need," responded Hazen.

"It's really just a matter of looking around and being aware of where the boomers and their kids are in our world," I said. "Have you seen all the media hype about the new Coliseum that recently opened in Ottawa's west end?"

"No Roman gladiators at Ottawa's Coliseum — only Hollywood movies and plenty of boomer families," replied Hazen, chuckling. "That's another good example of a company catering to the boomer family. Famous Players is firing on all of the demographic cylinders. With a 12-screen cinema that offers something to every member of the family — comfortable seating for mom and dad, video arcades for their kids — they've designed a facility where every member of the family comes early, stays late and spends a lot of money. Famous Players knows that their key demographic — boomers and their teenage kids — are at a stage in their lives where they're ready to leave the nest and go outside the home for their entertainment. The film-exhibition industry will be worth about $700 million this year alone. As the boomers and their kids age, the industry has been seeing at least 10 percent increases in its growth each year. That's the power of demographics."

"And there's plenty more examples out there, Hazen. Look at these laser eye surgery clinics. How about all these new cruise ships I see advertised? What about all the hype about menopause and now manopause? Look at the horde of boomers cruising the highways in their sport utility vehicles — the van is dead as a dodo now. The boom is everywhere," I said, throwing up my hands.

"So, when are you ready to start?" Hazen asked. "You've just hit on several of the subjects I want to canvass for my new seminar. Let's get working."

That question took me by surprise. I'd thought my next job probably wouldn't be lined up until the kids started school in September. What was I going to do with them? Emily, at nine, was too young to be left on her own. I'd have to get a sitter or maybe arrange day camps for her. Malcolm, now 15, was old enough to look after himself, but he was also old enough to get into trouble if he spent a summer just hanging out with his buddies. In a way, I'd been looking forward to spending time with the kids over the summer. But at the same time, I couldn't turn down this opportunity. What a dilemma!

"What's the problem, Meredith?" asked Hazen. "You seem preoccupied."

"I am — a bit. I hate to sound unprofessional, but it's just that I've got to figure out what to do with my kids over the summer months."

"That shouldn't be so tough," Hazen answered. "You can work at home most days."

"Really? That would be great. And if that's the case, I could start as soon as you'd like. Hey, I'll be part of that trend of more and more Canadians working at home," I stated.

"Be careful how you use that word 'trend' and be

careful what you say about home offices," said Hazen. "In fact, that's another thing that I want you to research this summer — the difference between a fad and a trend. As Binney & Smith realized, the fact that Canada is short on young kids is not a fad, it's a trend. In the next few decades, there will probably be more deaths than there are births each year in this country. I think that the ability to discern between a fad and a trend is the key to successful long-term investing. And the distinction becomes even more acute when you factor in the baby boomers, pushing themselves in and out of markets."

"What do you mean?" I had a feeling my new job had already begun — and I didn't even know how much I was going to earn on this contract!

"Long-term investors want to identify trends — things that are going to stay with us for a good long time," Hazen replied.

"And home offices aren't a trend? I thought they were all the rage," I said.

"You're right. In fact, well over two million Canadians work at home these days and many are self-employed. Technologies like the computer and fax machines have allowed many jobs to leave the office environment and move home. But I sense a backlash against home offices. People are finding that working at home is not all it's cracked up to be," Hazen explained.

"Why is that?" I asked, now questioning my decision to work at home over the summer.

"First, you have to examine the reasons why people work out of their houses," began Hazen. "Many workers don't want to be at home — they were downsized out of the economy or their employer doesn't want to pay for office space for them. Others may have wanted to try working from home, but they've found it tough. It's lonely and difficult to escape work when it's actually sitting in your house. In fact, the author of a book I was reading the other day called *Career Intelligence* argues that home offices can increase stress. Some home workers sense a loss of their personal sanctuary. 'When your whole house becomes your office, you can never leave the office — and you can never come home,' the writer observed."

"That doesn't sound too appealing," I agreed, wondering how I'd manage.

"So, when the employment situation improves, like it's doing right now, I think we're going to see more than a few at-home workers returning to their office desks. Then look at the demographics. The number of women working at home has increased by nearly 70 percent over the past decade. And many of those women are like you, Meredith — they're working at home because they've got young children. What happens when the kids grow up? I'd guess many of those women will want to get out of the house at that point."

"Meaning this may be a mere fad masquerading as a trend," I said.

"It means we have to examine not only the numbers but also the reasons why something is happening," he replied. "Looking only at the numbers, it appears that home offices are a booming, long-term trend. But, digging deeper, it may be that the anticipated growth in home offices simply won't materialize."

Out of the corner of my eye, I saw Pieter appear at our front door and begin his search for the newspaper.

"Pieter — over here!" I shouted, waving. I glanced at my watch. Emily had a swimming lesson at eleven, so I'd better get back home. Plus, I was eager to tell Pieter the good news about my job. I began gathering my coffee things together. "Well, time to get on with my day, Hazen. I guess I'll see you Monday morning. Oh, before I leave, do you know the line 'What is so rare as a day in June?' " That quotation was still wandering around in my head, like a tune you just can't shake. If anybody would know the author it would be Hazen.

"James Russell Lowell, an American poet," he replied without hesitation. "It was in a poem about the legend of the Holy Grail. Let me see if I can remember the title." He paused. "I studied it back in my university days. Just a second — 'The Vision of Sir Launfal.' Yes, that's it." He sat back in his chair, obviously satisfied with his memory.

"Sort of like *The Last Crusade.* Did you ever see that Indiana Jones movie? Or how about that Monty Python flick, *The Search for the Holy Grail?*" My cultural references weren't quite as highfalutin as Hazen's.

"It's interesting you mention those two movies. The search for the grail is seen as the object of a long and difficult quest. That's what we are just about to do — embark on a challenging search for information. Are we ready?" he asked.

"Let's go."

2

Something New Under the Sun

When I arrived home from taking Emily to her Saturday-morning swimming lesson, I noticed the light flashing on our answering machine.

"Meredith, it's Hazen here. I know it's a late invitation, but are you and Pieter busy tonight? Ruth is coming over for an early dinner and I wondered if the two of you might join us. Give me a call when you get back in."

Pieter and I had no plans for the evening. Lately, our weeknights had been action packed and we looked forward to not doing much on the weekends. I'd vaguely thought about heading over to Blockbuster to see if I could rent *The Full Monty* — we must be the only people in Ottawa who haven't seen it. The kids had their own plans; they seemed to have more active social lives than Pieter and I these days. Emily was off for a sleepover birthday party at Janine's, and Malcolm was heading out to the movies with his buddies. Dinner at Hazen's sounded good. I always came away from an evening with Ruth and Hazen feeling I'd learned something useful. The best part was, I never knew what I'd learn, I never felt I was being lectured to and we always shared a few good laughs along the way.

Where had Pieter gone off to? Before I phoned Hazen, I wanted to see what my husband thought about the invitation. He could sometimes be prickly about these things. Socializing wasn't as easy for Pieter as it was for me. Even after 17 years of marriage, I couldn't always predict his reactions. I knew that, like me, he enjoyed spending time with Hazen and Ruth. They'd been up to our cottage together and we had marvellous times. But I also knew Pieter had been feeling stressed about work recently. He'd emerged from a stretch of too little work and plunged into a period of far too much and was really pressed for time. He might just prefer an evening of crashing on the couch with a movie.

It still amazed me, after all these years together, how different we were in many ways. Yet for each difference, there was a profound similarity. Different, but the same. Maybe that's what kept our marriage going. We combined stability with a bit of spice.

So, where was Pieter anyway? I wanted to get back to Hazen before it was too late in the afternoon.

As I plunked my purse on the kitchen counter, I caught sight of a yellow sticky note on the door of the microwave. Pieter leaves notes in the weirdest places!

"Malcolm and I have gone to the bike store. No need to call Hazen back. I bumped into him on our way out and said yes. Knew you'd love to see Ruth. Back at 4:00 or so. I love you. Pieter P.S. I said we'd bring a salad. Will pick up the stuff on my way home. P."

And there I was being so thoughtful and he just went ahead and accepted without asking me. The bum! Well, I guess I discovered another difference between Pieter and me! And what was the problem, really? We both ended up with what we wanted. Don't sweat the small stuff. Pieter's always saying that to me. All's well that ends well, right?

I had just come in from uprooting some gigantic dandelions from the garden when I heard Malcolm and Pieter unlocking the front door.

"So, how's the bike?" I called.

"We left it at the store," answered Pieter, walking into the kitchen and dropping two grocery bags onto the counter.

"Yeah, I bent my front wheel riding in Gatineau Park this morning, and Dad says I have to pay for the repair." added Malcolm. "It's gonna be 60 bucks — to fix a bent front wheel!"

"Sounds as if you better hunt around for some babysitting jobs," I said. "With the going rates these days, you'll only need to take a couple of jobs."

"Yeah, yeah. I've heard it already, Mom: 'You've got to take responsibility for your own stuff.' Dad already gave me the lecture on the way home," replied Malcolm, heading upstairs. What had happened to this kid? Gone was the sweet little boy who was always eager to pitch in and help. In his place was a teenager whose primary occupation was hanging out with his friends and barely acknowledging his parents.

"It's not what he says that bugs me, it's the tone of voice he uses," I commented to Pieter once Malcolm was out of earshot.

"That's part of being a teenager, honey. Don't get caught up in the details. He's doing well in school, he's got good friends, he's basically a good kid. A lot of what's going on here is part of the normal growing-up process. He's separating from us and developing his own life. Cut him a bit of slack, okay?"

"I know you're right," I said. "It's stressful, that's all. And I know from the research I did for Ruth that there are plenty of families in the same boat as we are. Nearly 40 percent of parents with teens say their kids cause them more stress than their spouse, employers, parents or friends. In fact, many boomers are in for a pretty wild time with their kids — the echo generation — as they head into their teens."

"You've learned a lot over the past couple of years. Working with Ruth was a great opportunity for you," replied Pieter. He began pulling salad ingredients out of the shopping bags. "How about I get the veggies organized and you make that great vinaigrette from *The Silver Palate*?"

"Okay, it's a deal. You're right, you know. I know a lot more about our generation than I give myself credit for. Here's the amazing thing — I've got this growing feeling that all this information is leading me somewhere. It's helped me out in my own life. I know that I'm not alone facing the issues we're dealing with as a family. The majority of families around us are wrestling with the same issues: aging parents, teenagers, the time crunch, saving for kids' schooling, thinking about our health, preparing for retirement. I feel I'm finally starting to get it," I explained, searching the shelves for my cookbook.

Pieter looked up from the sink and turned off the water, then grabbed a handful of paper towels to dry the lettuce. "I think that's part of being middle-aged. It's like a football game. The first half is over, we've reviewed our strategy at halftime and now we're ready to hit the field again. We've run good and hard, we've been tackled a couple of times, taken a few shots, and maybe we've even been lucky enough to score a touchdown, but we've all learned something while playing the game and moving through our lives." Pieter chuckled. "At least, I hope we have."

"I think people could benefit from learning about the research I've seen while working with Ruth. As many boomers hit middle age, they start considering how their lives fit together. They're worried about things. Are they doing the things they really want to do? Do they have the time to enjoy life? How do they want to tackle the second half? Aging is tough for a generation of boomers raised to idealize youth. They don't know how to age gracefully. Look at the statistics on cosmetic surgery, for example. Did you know that the number of liposuction procedures jumped by approximately 300 percent in the past five years? Remember all those books I got out of the library last month about simplifying your life, finding balance, that sort of stuff?" I asked.

Pieter nodded. "I thought you found all those books frustrating."

"I did. They had some really goofy suggestions in them, like buying a plastic baseball bat and slugging your pillows. That was supposed make you feel better. Wouldn't work for me. But that's not the point. There's a big market for books like that because people want to make sense of life. I think it would really help people to know *why* they're feeling the way they are these days," I said.

"I'm not sure I follow you," replied Pieter. "Give me an example."

"Well, look at us. We were in a real muddle when we moved to this house. Our finances were in a mess. We were stressed out. Neither one of us was happy. It was only after we met Hazen, and started understanding what had happened to us and why, that we were able to begin rebuilding our lives in a meaningful way by developing a life plan."

"Getting our finances in order was a big help," Pieter acknowledged.

"But it's not only us who are having a hard time with their finances. Did you see that article in yesterday's paper about Canadians and retirement? It was a survey for the accounting firm Deloitte & Touche. Evidently, the majority of Canadians are headed towards a low-income retirement unless they change their savings habits. As it stands today, they're not saving enough. In fact, that's one topic I'm going to be researching for Hazen this summer. It's not only the DeMarcos who are worried about money," I said.

"I'd agree with that. But how does that fit in with those books telling boomers how to balance their lives?"

"I think if we all spent less time hitting pillows with

plastic baseball bats and a bit more time thinking about getting our financial and emotional houses in order, we'd find a lot more balance in our lives. And we'd feel a whole lot better about what life had in store for us as we headed back out for the second half of that game you were talking about," I replied.

"It's too bad everybody can't have someone like Hazen in their lives," commented Pieter. He was searching the drawers for a paring knife.

"But that's just it. They can!" I answered. "And I think I know how to make it happen. Ruth and Hazen need to get together. Here are two experts working on the same basic topic — the baby boomers. They both understand that boomers set the agenda in this country, but they're coming at that topic from different directions. Ruth has done all this interesting research into the current mindset of the boomers, our generational emotional state and the reasons we think the way we do. Hazen works from a different angle, helping boomers get their finances in shape by analyzing their impact on the economy and our financial markets. We know from our own experience that you can't have one without the other. It's tough keeping your emotions on an even keel when your finances are a wreck. Life isn't really complete until these two pieces of the puzzle — emotions and finances — come together. So, if Ruth and Hazen could bring their work together, I think boomers would be pretty interested in the result," I concluded.

"Are you suggesting they write a book together?" Pieter asked.

"Well, Ruth is a talented writer, and Hazen's reworking

his seminar — with my help. A book is a definite possibility," I replied.

Pieter glanced at his watch. "Let's concentrate on the task at hand and get finished with this salad. Hazen has invited us for six o'clock. You'll have the perfect opportunity to suggest the book idea tonight."

"I'd feel like I was meddling," I said. "Let me think about it."

"Meredith, it's a great idea," he said. "Who knows? You could be the conduit to bring their work together. Give it a shot."

At about four-thirty, I noticed Ruth's car parked outside Hazen's house. When I asked Pieter if he was certain about the time of the invitation, he glared at me and reminded me once again not to get caught up in the details. I arrived at Hazen's promptly at six, salad in hand. Ruth answered the door.

"I thought we had the time wrong," I said as I entered the front hall. "I saw your car here over an hour ago."

"Hazen and I were having a family powwow," she replied quietly, shaking her head. I could tell something was bothering her. "Where's Pieter?" she asked, glancing behind me.

"Malcolm and his buddies cajoled him into driving them to the movies. He'll be here in 15 minutes or so. Ruth, that's the first time I've heard you refer to you and Hazen as a family. What's going on?"

We were interrupted by Hazen, who began shouting from the kitchen.

"This time it's different!" he yelled.

"What are you muttering about?" Ruth said. "More cooking, less talking!"

Hazen popped his head out of the kitchen. "No, this is really important. This is work. I've decided to call my new seminar 'This Time It's Different.' And I wanted to tell Meredith the good news."

"Good news?" said Ruth sarcastically. "Say that about the stock markets and you're guaranteed to hear more than a few snorts of derision. That's the sort of thing over-eager brokers say when a market at all-time highs is poised to plunge. You're tempting fate, Hazen!"

"Exactly," he said. "I want to be provocative. I want to challenge the audience."

"But are you right? Is it ever different? My uncle Jack loves to quote Ecclesiastes: 'That which has been is what will be, that which is done will be done, and there is nothing new under the sun,'" Ruth challenged, hands on hips. Ruth's uncle had taken on legendary proportions in her life. Now well into his nineties, Jack, a Montreal rabbi, had long served as Ruth's spiritual mentor. Her conversation was colourfully spiced with Jack's aphorisms, his Yiddish wisdom.

"Right again. I'd agree with that too," said Hazen. "I'm certainly not going to disagree with either wise preacher, Jack or Ecclesiastes. It seems to me I've heard Jack often say, 'In a quarrel, each side is right.'"

"Okay, you two. One at a time," I interrupted. "Hazen, it sounds as if you're arguing both sides of the story here. What is 'This Time It's Different' all about? I want to know more about what I'm going to be working on this summer."

"We've seen profound changes in our economy over the past decade," explained Hazen. He rhymed off his list on his fingers. "First, the battle to beat inflation appears to have been won. The push is on for governments around the world to become fiscally responsible — and they're doing it. Look at our own government's victory over the deficit. For the first time since 1974, Canada will have not only a balanced budget but a surplus to boot. Second, interest rates are as low as they've been in our memory. In the long term, there's no push for them to go higher. Third, factor in our recent technological progress. We're going from an economy that relies on railroads, steel companies and brawn to one that counts on microchips, fibre optics and the human brain. In Ontario, for example, knowledge- and technology-based industries are the source of two out of every three new jobs. Between 1992 and 1997, Canada recorded an over 90 percent increase in the number of computer programming and systems analyst jobs. Pretty amazing!"

"I'd agree there have been big changes in the economy. But how does that make it different this time?" I asked. Ruth held a bottle of white wine aloft, offering me a glass. "Thanks, Ruth."

"Would you mind pouring me a glass too? I'm just warming up to my topic here," said Hazen. "The big difference is what economists call the 'smoothing out' of the business cycle. The business cycle refers to the ups and downs in economic activity over a period of years. At the peak of the cycle, the economy is at full employment, output is at capacity. The trough, on the other hand, is the bottom of the cycle — employment and capacity hit their lowest levels. The most dramatic example, of course, is the trough experienced during the Great Depression."

"And," interrupted Ruth, "if memory serves me right, the prognosticators were saying 'this time it's different' right up to the day of the crash in 1929."

"Right again. The big difference now is that our business cycle has flattened out considerably since the 1930s. The rhythm of business activity has altered significantly over the past 70 years. We are moving away from having heavy manufacturing industries at the centre of our economy. According to Statistics Canada, service industries — business services, communications, transportation, accommodation — are the fastest-growing sectors in our economy. And they rely on human capital, not huge capital outlays like the industries of yesteryear. As a result, we're not going to see the gigantic investment surges we did when railroads were built across this country, or highways constructed or cities of skyscrapers erected. From here on, growth is going to be slower and steadier. That means the business cycles won't pack the punch they once did. We won't see the highs we once did but, fortunately, we won't see the lows either. And that's good for the economy."

"Could we use the recession in the early 1990s as an example of that smoothing out of the cycle?" I asked. "It was both shorter and milder than the one in the 1980s."

"It was definitely different," Hazen answered. "It also serves as a good example of how the government has changed its response to troughs in the business cycle. Instead of spending its way out of the recession, the government allowed the economy to right itself. Many would argue this indicates the economy is better managed now. That's different too."

Ruth assumed the role of devil's advocate. "But, Hazen, you haven't once mentioned your favourite topic, the baby boom. Where do they fit into your new and different world?"

"Ah, they're at centre stage, actually," Hazen replied, peering into the oven. "Okay — everything is set in the kitchen. We've got about 20 minutes before dinner's ready. Let's move into the living room for my pièce de résistance."

"Oh, brother," Ruth muttered to me. "He thinks he's too smart by half. Let's not let him get away with this." She was looking at me as she said these words, but they were obviously directed at Hazen. He smiled smugly as he ushered the two of us into his "gentlemen's club" living room.

Once we were settled, Hazen resumed his commentary. "We'd be wise to consider the long-term motivation of the boomers. They're approaching their prime income and investing years, so they have the money to invest. This is where I'd agree with Ecclesiastes — there is nothing new under the sun. People age and they start preparing for their golden years. It's a very predictable process. And where are they investing? These days, what with low interest rates and inflation, there's one very appealing place to put that cash — the stock market. When rates are low, it makes less sense to invest in a fixed-rate investment like a GIC with its rate stuck in the basement. Bonds, with their fixed yields, may have similar problems and, as a result, have lost their lustre. The

Investment Funds Institute of Canada reported that as Canadians stay away from bonds and banks, sales of equity mutual funds have been averaging close to $1 billion a week over the past couple of months."

"If they're no different from their predecessors," asked Ruth, "how do you know the boom generation is not going to get scared out of the market when the inevitable correction comes along? Most of today's investors have never seen anything but a bull market. What happens when the bears come out to play?"

"There's no denying that there will be corrections along the way, but this is 'patient' capital, looking to the long term and unperturbed by short-term volatility in the stock market, especially when the alternatives are offering paltry rates of return. Boomers have 20 to 30 years before retirement. And don't forget that boomers invest in the market very differently — another difference! — from previous generations. Instead of simply holding stocks directly, they hold shares indirectly, through mutual funds that invest all or part of their holdings in stocks. In fact, since 1989, the percentage of direct shareholders in the Toronto Stock Exchange has decreased by more than 25 percent, while the percentage of shareholders who own both shares and mutual funds has increased by nearly 90 percent.

"Plus, much of the money invested in the stock market is currently in RRSPs, which by their very nature are long-term investments. A majority of the investors in the TSE cite long-term gains, such as building a retirement fund, as the main reason for investing in the market. Combine all this with the fact that boomers are becoming increasingly well educated about financial investments and the natural ups and downs of the market, and we've got a different group of investors this time, the type that can weather a correction or two. Look, these investors have had the benefit of a bit of education. I saw an article in the *Globe and Mail* just the other day advising investors to resist the urge to push the investment panic button when markets decline. In fact, the article presented a market correction as the perfect time to buy more stocks and rejig your portfolio. Oh, investors will certainly be nervous when they see the value of their portfolios drop. Hey, we're currently riding the greatest bull market of the century. More than a few investors don't know what it's like to watch the value of their stocks decline. But when the inevitable bear shows his face, I predict that the vast majority of investors in this market will not panic."

"So what happens," asked Ruth, "when it comes time for the baby boomers to retire and cash out of the stock market? That's the next logical question. What's different there?"

"A baby boomer, who only spent *one* year in Grade 2 and owned only *one* family home at a time, looks differently at the bond and stock market — stocks and bonds are for accumulating and hoarding. A boomer will keep her Nortel stocks while acquiring shares in Bombardier. And that process still has many years to run. The oldest boomers won't be ready for retirement until the 2010s. People tend to keep accumulating assets and increasing their net worth until they're nearly 70, so the oldest boomers won't start cashing in their investments until well into the 2010s. And then? Well, I'm not predicting a crash," stated Hazen.

"But there is going to be turmoil in the markets," I said. "After all, the boomers are going to want their money, right?"

"We'll definitely see a few corrections along the way. But that's a normal market phenomenon. The boom stretches over almost 20 years — the oldest are now just over 50 and the youngest in their mid-thirties. So the sell-off will occur at a slow, steady pace during which we'll see boomers move their investments to less-risky stocks and income-producing assets," explained Hazen. "And don't forget a couple of fundamental differences in our world. People are living longer than ever before. Back in the 1920s, life expectancy at birth was less than 60 years for a man. Today, it's nearly 75 for males, 80 for females. We're going to need to have our money invested and earning if we expect to have sufficient funds to see us through those long — and, hopefully, productive — lives. And speaking of productive, all this blither about early retirement is just that. Boomers have plans to work well past retirement age. Hey, they're going to be healthy and they want to keep active. Why not keep bringing home the bacon at the same time? A recent U.S. study by the American Association of Retired Persons indicated that 80 percent of boomers plan to work past 65. That will also slow the sell-off of stocks filling the boomers' portfolios."

"But, Hazen, don't we need to look longer term?" I asked. "What happens when the companies that the boomers hold in their stock portfolios don't have anybody to sell to?" I knew from studying with Ruth that

Canada faced a slowing population growth due to low fertility and the aging of the baby-boom generation. How could North American companies sustain the growth they needed to continue their profitable ways?

"Thank you, Meredith. You've brought me to possibly the biggest difference. And this time it's really different. It's time to broaden our discussion from North American demographics to global demographics. Approximately 95 percent of the world's population lives outside this continent, so we better pay attention. The emerging nations have very large, very young populations. And, like it or not, we now live in a global village. The rest of the world wants what we have. The result? This huge young generation is very interested in our consumer products. Companies like Coca-Cola and Gillette are already riding the global population wave, and plenty more are poised to catch that wave. It's a different but very good time for many North American companies."

Ruth was smiling. "Hold it, Hazen. You've focused on differences. But at the outset of this discussion you acknowledged there is nothing new under the sun. Let's hear the other side of your argument."

"A couple of things," Hazen replied. "It all leads straight back to the stock market. All this change in our economy has simply reinforced the advisability of investing in the stock market. It's the best place for a long-term investor to be. It's the stable place in a changing world. The proof lies in an examination of the historical evidence. In his book *Stocks for the Long Run*, Jeremy Siegel reviews the U.S. financial market returns since 1802. The results are stunning. His research demonstrates that the returns on equities have surpassed those on other financial assets over long periods. But there's more. Stock returns were actually more predictable than bond returns when examined in light of their purchasing power. That means that the first choice for any long-term investor should be the stock market. Stability in a sea of change."

"You're forgetting one important constant in a new and different world," added Ruth.

"What's that?" asked Hazen.

"The ability of people not only to adapt to change but to thrive — to take new ideas, new inventions, and apply their imaginations to use those ideas and inventions for the benefit of all of us," said Ruth. "Look at electricity. It transformed the lives of the generations before us. My grandmother washed clothes by hand. My mother started married life with an old wringer washer. And I've got a state-of-the-art Maytag washer-and-dryer combo that does everything but put the clothes away in the drawer. The same thing is happening now with computer technology. We're living in revolutionary times, and it's a testament to the human spirit that we can win the revolution every time."

"I like that. Thank you, Ruth," Hazen said with a smile. "What do you think, Meredith? We've got our work cut out for us, don't we?"

"I think we can use some of the ideas Ruth and I researched to expand on the differences you see in the financial markets. Differences that go a long way to explaining why things are different now," I commented.

"Can you give me some examples off the top of your head?" Hazen asked.

"Help me out on this," I said, looking at Ruth.

She chuckled. "You're on your own here. Let's see what you learned."

"Well," I started tentatively, "we're living longer, healthier lives than ever before." Out of the corner of my eye, I saw Ruth nodding. "We've been transformed from a rural to an urban society. Look back a hundred years — 75 percent of Canadians lived in rural settings. Now, more than 75 percent live in cities. In recent years, women have taken on new and different roles in society. They've entered the workforce in unprecedented numbers, transforming many professions. Here's an example: the younger the doctor, the better chance she is a woman. More than half the doctors in Canada under the age of 30 are women. Working women have also transformed family life. In approximately seven of every ten Canadian couples, both spouses work. That was unheard of in my mother's day. This has not only changed the balance of power within the family but it's also created new pressures. The time crunch is a good example of the type of pressures many families now face. And don't forget education. The boomers were much better educated than their parents. That's made huge changes. I'd bet you could argue that one of the reasons the computer revolution has been so successful is that we've had such a well-educated generation of boomers who were capable of applying this technology in both their work and personal lives."

"Yes," said Hazen, "I can see how we'll be able to work those ideas into the seminar. What else were you thinking about, Meredith?"

The doorbell sounded. Saved by the bell and Pieter! His arrival gave me a few minutes to collect my thoughts. What else could I add?

"Did you get the boys dropped off?" I asked Pieter as he walked into the room.

He smiled. "They wanted to go way out to that new Coliseum place. That's why I'm so late. Sorry."

"No, don't apologize," replied Hazen. "Meredith and I were talking about that cinema just yesterday. Sounds like a real mecca for boomers and their kids. Maybe the four of us should take a little field trip out there this summer, investigate the demographics and catch a movie at the same time. While you were chauffeuring your kids, Meredith was making a few suggestions for our work together. Very interesting ideas."

"You were quick, Meredith. So, you told them about your book idea." Pieter looked at me eagerly.

"Book idea?" Ruth said. "No, we were talking about Hazen and Meredith's work on the seminar. Are you planning on writing a book, Meredith?"

Pieter gave me a guilty look. Well, fools rush in where angels dare to tread. May as well get it over with, I thought.

"No," I said slowly, "no, I'm not writing a book. I think that the two of you should write a book. Something that does exactly what we were doing just now. It could weave together the social and financial changes heralded in by the baby-boom generation. You know that Pieter and I have always referred to you collectively as the 'Boom Doctors.' Why not go public with your routine?" I challenged.

Hazen and Ruth stared at one another. Both were silent for several seconds.

"Actually, that's not a bad idea," said Hazen.

"Better caution at first than tears afterwards — my uncle Jack says that," Ruth began gingerly. "It is a good idea. I do have my sabbatical coming up in September, and you're busy squirrelling away new research material for your seminar. The timing is perfect. I guess it's something worth thinking about. What do you say, Hazen?"

"For once, I agree with your uncle Jack," he replied. We all laughed. "But I do think we should spend some time this summer thinking about it. This could really work."

"And they're off," Pieter said to me in a soft aside. "Good work."

3

Avoid the Noise

"I'm heading over to the grocery store," I announced. "Anybody want to come along?" We had just finished lunch and the kids were busy clearing the table.

Pieter looked up from the newspaper spread open on the dining-room table. He appeared set for the afternoon, coffee in one hand, a stack of weekend papers at the other. "Why are you going for groceries on Sunday? I thought you did your big shopping on Wednesdays."

"How quickly we forget," I replied. "I'm a working woman again. I'm going to be busy from here on in. If the shopping doesn't get done today, we won't eat next week. I know you're a hi-tech guy, Pete, but there are some basics in this world. If you don't eat, you die."

"Mom, I can't help," Emily shouted from the kitchen. "I'm going over to Rachel's this afternoon. We're working on our book reports. It's our last project before the end of school."

"Well, I guess that lets you off the hook, sweetie," I said. Mention a chore and the rats leap off the ship in very short order. "What about you, Malcolm? I could use some help carrying the groceries home."

"I'm busy and I'm going out," he replied curtly. "I don't want to help anyway."

Here we go again, I thought. I exchanged glances with Pieter.

"Look, Malcolm, I spoke to you politely. I expect a polite response," I said evenly. "You don't have to help, but I do want you to finish cleaning up here, and you're on deck for setting the table for supper." No response. I walked into the kitchen. "Malcolm, did you hear me?"

"Yeah. Okay, I'll set the table," he answered, keeping his back to me as he spoke. "I think I'll go play basketball with the guys this afternoon. I've got all my homework done."

"That sounds fine," I said.

"He's definitely a teenager," chuckled Pieter once the kids had finished in the kitchen and gone upstairs. "You handled that pretty well, keeping your eye on the big picture and not getting bogged down in winning the little skirmish. You can lose the battle and still win the war, you know."

"It's hard to do all the time. It's tiring and sometimes I don't have much patience for it, that's all. It would be so much easier if things were the way they used to be. And I can tell that you're not going to help me out with the shopping either."

"Nope. I'm going to read this afternoon. I'll tell you what — how about I do the groceries next Sunday?"

"You've got a deal," I said, searching the kitchen counter for my grocery list.

Bank Street slices the Glebe in half. Hank's Hardware, McKnight's grocery store, the pharmacy, a couple of bakeries, bookstores, butchers, restaurants, clothing stores and a gaggle of coffee shops line the street. Everyone in our neighbourhood ends up on Bank Street a couple of times each week at least. Today was no different. Teenagers on skateboards, young couples pushing strollers, kids walking dogs, elderly couples out for an afternoon stroll. Stopping to say hi to one of Emily's friends, I also spotted my around-the-corner neighbour walking on the other side of the street. We exchanged waves. This street is what I love about my neighbourhood — the sense of community, the coziness of the place.

As I walked past the Second Cup, I noticed Hazen sitting in the window, half reading, half people watching. I knocked on the window. He smiled and gestured for me to come in.

"Hey, this is a nice way to spend the afternoon," I said. "What are you reading?"

"It's called *Market Magic: Riding the Greatest Bull Market of the Century.*"

"That sounds up your alley."

"The author — her name is Louise Yamada; she's a technical analyst with Salomon Smith Barney, a large brokerage firm in the U.S. — bases her perspective on the market on demographics, both national and global. Very interesting stuff. She feels that we're in the middle of the third great bull market of the twentieth century with potential to extend into the twenty-first century. She examines world demographics and concludes that successful companies will be those that market around the globe. She also believes that the future belongs to companies that are constantly improving their products and developing new ones. 'Like money, technology changes everything,' she writes. She's convinced that technology will alter life as we know it as our economic landscape evolves from heavy industrial to information-based. As a result, she argues, 'the role of the natural resources of the old industrial age will be greatly altered, as water, for instance, rises to rival oil and gold.'"

"Water more valuable than gold? That's wild," I said.

"'Water, water, everywhere, nor any drop to drink,' Coleridge wrote prophetically back in the 1700s," replied Hazen, flipping through the book. "Here," he began, "Yamada writes that 'water is the most valuable finite resource on the globe — the necessity of life. Yet water is already scarce today, with shortages in 80 countries affecting 40 percent of the world's population.' We sometimes lose sight of what's happening beyond our borders, and drinking water is an increasingly valuable commodity. As for a commodity like gold, well, it looks great as jewellery but its days as an investment commodity may be over. People look at the U.S. dollar as the world's unit of exchange these days. This time some things *are* different, and we can't let our vision become narrowed to the possibilities the world has to offer." He chuckled.

"I've never thought about water that way. Sounds interesting," I commented.

"The book is great, but I must admit that I'm having trouble concentrating on it. Here," said Hazen, pulling out the chair beside him. "Why don't you sit down?"

"I could tell," I replied, sliding into the seat. "You were people watching when I walked by."

"Excuse me, that was serious research. I've seen four golden retrievers walk by this window with owners in tow. This confirms what I've read about pet ownership in this country. Did you know that over the past 20 years, we've doubled our spending on pets?"

"I'm not surprised. Have you seen those pet superstores springing up all over town?"

Hazen grinned. "It's the boomers at work. Pet owners are more likely to be homeowners with kids. Does this sound like a generation you know? In fact, when I was down in New York recently, I walked by Wagging Tail Doggie Daycare, a storefront filled with indulged pooches right in the middle of Manhattan. Boomers have really gone to the dogs! Look," Hazen said excitedly, pointing across the street at a young couple walking a golden retriever. "There's another one as we speak!" We both laughed. "Why don't you join me for a quick coffee? I've got a couple of work things to bounce off you. Let me buy."

"Okay, but I can't stay long. I've got grocery shopping to do this afternoon." We went over to the counter. As I was making my selection — way too many choices in these coffee shops — Hazen began to speak.

"Actually, I was pondering more than dogs. I was also thinking about Dylan. He and I had an interesting discussion — a quarrel, really — this morning. He called from California. He's just finished up an undergraduate math degree at UCLA, and he's decided to take a year off before pursuing his graduate studies."

"That doesn't sound bad. So what did you fight about?" I asked.

"It seems that he doesn't want to do anything during this year off," Hazen replied. "He wants to come back here and spend some time with Ruth and me. He's thinking about working as a waiter. He tells me that his real reason for coming home is his concern that Ruth and I are drifting apart without him around. He said something about getting our family together — before it was too late. I told him he's going to lose his edge, miss out on getting into graduate school if he takes it easy for a year. He didn't want to hear that."

"If it's any consolation, I just came from a war of words with Malcolm. He's been giving me a hard time these past few months. It's tough being a parent."

"Boomers are poised to find that out," said Hazen. "The boomers' kids are growing up. We're going to see an explosion in the number of teenagers. Those tweens that we were talking about yesterday will be thinking of driving in a couple of years. The echo boom generation, the boomers' kids born after 1980, are some seven million strong in Canada. The big retailers have already caught on to this — take a look at the Gap, for example. It operates about 2,200 stores worldwide, filled with the midpriced line of clothing that kids love. And because it's not totally outrageous stuff, the Gap sells to the parents of those kids too."

"You're right. These khakis came from the Gap's sale rack," I said.

"Did you know that the Gap refers to the generation gap? The first store opened back in 1969 and traded on the difference between the boomers and their parents. No self-respecting 1960s mom and dad wore Levi's! Ironically, the Gap has made its fortune selling across the generations. People of all ages — all of whom worship the youth culture of our society — shop at the Gap these days. Boomers blazed the trail in bringing down the walls that previously separated the generations."

"Be careful with predicting the shopping patterns of teens, Hazen. I know from experience that echo kids are very brand-conscious. Hey, you're a teenaged nobody unless you've got a pair of Mantras, NFAs, a pair of DCs and a really good set of Destructo trucks," I said.

"Pardon me?"

"Sunglasses, jeans, shoes and the axles of a skateboard. At a cool $500, that's what you need to be a boarder in this town," I explained.

The counter clerk called out my order — a small decaf caffe latte.

"You've raised another good point," Hazen said as I returned, coffee in hand. "Like we mentioned yesterday, these kids are flush with cash — money from indulgent grandparents and babysitting can add up when you have no expenses besides skateboard paraphernalia. Back when Dylan was a baby, Ruth and I paid neighbourhood kids 50 cents an hour to babysit. What does Malcolm bill out at?"

"His best customers pay him five dollars an hour."

"Well, the consumer price index today is about four times what it was back in the mid-1970s. That means that Malcolm should be looking at about two dollars per hour. See what happens when all those baby-boomer parents start competing for sitters for their little darlings?"

I laughed. "As long as my kid is reaping the benefits."

"This group of teens has spending power to spare and they'll be driving the fortunes of many companies in the apparel, entertainment and toy industries for the foreseeable future."

"I wouldn't want to try to sell to them," I replied. "They're so fickle at that age. And if something is uncool, well, that's the kiss of death."

"Just ask Levi Strauss & Co. about that. The brand of jeans that no self-respecting boomer could live without has been snubbed by the current crop of teens. Levi's has taken a beating, courtesy of teens' indifference to their jeans. Ten years ago, the company held a healthy 30 percent share of the U.S. blue-jean market. That's dropped to under 20 percent today. Why? Levi's focused their marketing on the adult market. They fell asleep at the switch when it came to teens. Now they're furiously updating their products and advertising to target this lucrative market. 'As the echo boom generation goes, so goes Levi Strauss & Co.,' said a Levi's executive recently. They've recognized the power of the babies of the boomers."

"But Levi's and the Gap only have to *sell* to these kids; we have to raise them. And it's not easy parenting a teen," I moaned.

"Hey, I remember those days. I had a teenager once. Remember when Malcolm was in his terrible twos? You ain't seen nothing. I can vouch for that. We had our share of issues with Dylan." He chuckled. "And it doesn't look as if it's over yet."

"But I read an article in the *Globe and Mail* recently that said that children of the boomers have more conservative family values than either their parents or grandparents. Evidently, they're true believers in the institution of marriage, for example. They're much more likely than their parents to want to tough out the rough spots in a marriage."

"Yes, I saw that article too," Hazen said. "It was based on StatsCan research. I'm not surprised by that reaction. Every generation says: 'This time will be different.'"

I smiled. "You're back to your theme of last evening."

"It's true, though. The children of the boomers watched their parents run through marriages like no generation before and they experienced the severe effects of divorce. Like any kids, they're critical of their parents — they see a self-indulgent generation of boomers and they're determined not to be like that. You see the same story repeated when you look at the statistics concerning volunteers: the rate of volunteerism among young adults has doubled over the past decade. We're getting into Ruth's territory here, but I see profound social change on the horizon."

"But isn't it natural for the younger generation to be more optimistic about the future than their parents? They haven't really experienced the school of hard knocks that maturing delivers. It's one thing to want a marriage to last; it's another to *make* it last. As for the volunteering, I think that many young volunteers see the benefits that they can reap from giving their time — unpaid work gives them an opportunity to get a toe into the job market while learning some new skills. I'm not so certain that we're on the verge of seeing a younger, kinder, gentler generation," I replied.

"All good points, Meredith," said Hazen thoughtfully. "And you're quite right, it pays to look at not only the statistics but also the stories behind those numbers."

"That still leaves us with the issues at hand," I responded. "Our kids are causing us stress here and now. We have to deal with those issues."

"The trick lies in avoiding the noise," said Hazen.

"What noise?"

"Parenting is like anything else. You have to keep your eye on the long run. Focus on the big picture."

"You sound exactly like Pieter. He keeps telling me not to get bogged in the details."

"He's right. We've got to look at the basic elements of our lives. Both of us have fundamentally good kids. In our daily hassles with them, we shouldn't lose sight of that. In fact, I want to use that phrase — 'avoid the noise' — in my new seminar. That advice applies to all areas of your life, including finances."

"In what context?"

"Well, Louise Yamada talks a bit in her book about avoiding the noise," Hazen said, patting the book on the table beside him. "Have you ever watched the business report on CNN or Newsworld?"

I nodded. "They're often a bit over my head, but after

our chats with you last year, I try to watch them periodically to keep abreast of what's going on in the world of business."

"The commentators are continually chattering about daily, weekly and monthly rates, numbers and statistics. One day they're in a flap about interest rates. Is Gordon Thiessen, the governor of the Bank of Canada, going to push the rate up tomorrow? The next, they're nattering about the inflation rate. How will today's U.S. unemployment statistics affect next month's inflation rate. Will what happened in Indonesia yesterday have any bearing on the TSE tomorrow? Is the dollar up or down today? What's the latest flash on Y2K? It's all noise. Yes, all those things might make for short-term changes in the markets. The TSE might rise 0.4 percent in a day on the news that Seagram purchased PolyGram, for example. Or it could fall when the pundits report that this month's inflation rate is infinitesimally higher than last month's. That's all short-term stuff."

"Yes, but it still makes the values of people's stocks go up and down," I replied. "That can be pretty nerve-racking for many folks."

Hazen chuckled. "That's why they've got to learn to avoid the noise. Yes, there will be big things that come along that affect the market. You pay attention to those things. But you have to be careful to differentiate the noise from the true shifts that do occur in our world. Here's a hint. The vast majority of what we see and hear is mere noise. Look, you're not even 40 yet. Just like many other boomers, you're investing your money for a good long time."

"Right," I interjected. "Pieter and I are preparing for our retirement years — and I'm reasonable enough not to expect 'Freedom 55.'"

"No kidding," said Hazen, smiling. "StatsCan just released a report predicting that, by 2015, workers who are over 55 will make up 20 percent of the workforce. That's up from 13 percent today. There won't be the pressure to downsize boomers out of the workforce. In fact, you'll be cherished in a way that your parents weren't. Because there's not a huge generation of younger workers nipping at your heels to get into the workforce, employers are going to need to keep you around, even when you start to get a bit long in the tooth."

"Okay, you made your point last night too — we're all going to be working past 65. So I won't be retiring for many, many years. You don't need to rub it in." We both laughed.

"Even though retirement is a long way off, you should still be focusing on building your portfolio for the time when you leave the workforce. That's not today, tomorrow, next week or next month. That's 25 years down the road, at least. Your view of the market's performance should be equally long term. The blips and jumps and tumbles the market takes along the way because of the daily noise of politics, economics and business shouldn't concern you," Hazen said.

"But what if the market plunges by 20 percent and I lose thousands of dollars in the value of my stock portfolio? That's going to give me a sleepless night or two."

"Fair enough. Of course that would concern you. But if you keep your eye on the long run, you would understand that the market is going to have corrections along the way. Corrections are a perfectly natural part of how the market operates. The trick is to ride out the bumps."

"But I've always heard that the way to do really well in the market is to buy low and sell high. So isn't the trick to figure out when those corrections will take place, sell just before they happen and then buy after the prices have fallen?" I asked.

"Tell me where you keep your crystal ball," Hazen said. "We all know corrections are going to happen. Timing them precisely is like predicting the future — not possible. And particularly not possible for ordinary folks like you and me. In fact, there is an investing strategy called 'market timing,' where investors sell in anticipation of a market downturn and buy when the market hits rock bottom. The problem is, market timing doesn't work too well for individual investors. Studies have shown that a greater risk than being caught in a market downturn is the risk of not being fully invested when the market comes back. If you look back at the history of the market, investors have earned higher total returns when they've remained fully invested."

"How can that be?" I asked.

"It's quite simple. Because they take their money *out* of the stock market, market timers miss out on unexpected high-performance days *in* the market. Let's say you had been investing $1,000 each year over the past 10 years in the TSE 300 index. If you stayed in that market every day over those 10 years, you would have pocketed an annualized compound return of about 10 percent. If you had tried your hand at market timing and missed the best 40 days — that's only 40 days over a 10-year period — your return would be a measly 2 percent per year," Hazen cautioned.

"So, it pays not to sweat the small stuff," I said.

"Exactly. But it's hard to communicate that message when people are fidgety and panicking about losing money in the markets." Hazen paused, holding his hands palms up in a gesture of bewilderment. "Nothing in life is certain, but there are a couple of known truths about the markets. In the short run — let's say you only hold your stocks for five years or less — stocks can be riskier than bonds or treasury bills. But contrast this with the long run. Let's look at a 20-year holding period, which is reasonable for a 40-year-old to contemplate. That's the example Jeremy Siegel gives in *Stocks for the Long Run.* From 1802 onwards, for holding periods of 20 years, stocks outperformed bonds and treasury bills more than 90 percent of the time. But investors who are familiar with that information can still become jittery, and want to pull out of the market, when they see the dollar swoon or interest rates hike up or an international crisis threatening. They sometimes lose sight of the fundamentals."

"I have an idea," I started excitedly. "Why don't you use an analogy. This happens to me every Friday in cottage season. I fret non-stop about the details of the day. How am I going to get everything ready — the grocery shopping, the kids' stuff, the car packed? I'm absolutely mired in the minutiae of the day. But then we arrive at the lake and we stroll down to the dock to watch the sun set. Life becomes reduced to its basic elements —

the sun, the lake, the loons. A huge weight lifts from my shoulders and I realize, then and there, what life's all about. The key, for me, is stepping back from all the crazy little details of my life and keeping my eye on the basics."

"That's wonderful imagery, Meredith. I think I *will* use that in my seminar. I like the word 'elements.' If we can break down our investing strategy into its fundamental elements, then we won't be shaken by market turmoil. And to think you weren't supposed to start work until tomorrow!"

"Speaking of which, what time do you want me?"

"I like to get going early. How about eight-thirty?"

"Sounds good. What will we be tackling?"

"One of the elemental items: the savings rate," replied Hazen. "It's amazing how many questions I get about the fact that Canada's savings rate is so low these days. In 1997, it fell to 2 percent, down from 4.5 percent in 1996 and nearly 7 percent in 1995. People want to know how we can have such a low savings rate and such a booming stock market."

"I can understand why they're puzzled. You argue that boomers' savings are what's driving the market. How can markets continue to go up when the savings rate keeps moving down?"

"That's what you're going to tell me," replied Hazen, smiling. "There are several very good explanations for this apparent conundrum. What I want you to do is review the relevant statistics and research and tell me, in a simple, straightforward way, why the boom is going to continue to be the driving force behind the market well into the 2000s. I'll incorporate your work into my seminar."

Simple? Straightforward? There didn't seem anything simple or straightforward about the financial markets. I wondered whether I was up to the task. I figured I may as well lay my cards on the table.

"Hazen, that sounds like a daunting job. I'm not sure I can handle it."

"Meredith, I have complete confidence in you. I've watched you and Pieter take control of your finances. I know you have a solid grasp of demographic issues from your work with Ruth. Plus, I'll give you some pointers on where to go and who to read. Hey, I'm starting you off with an easy issue."

"Okay, I'll believe you. But I think this is going to be more work than I envisioned. I'd better get going on this grocery shopping — I may not get back to a grocery store for the rest of the summer!"

Hazen chuckled. "Meredith, I guarantee that you'll find this work to be more interesting than the produce aisle at McKnight's," he said as I walked into the June sunshine.

I was into the home stretch, turning the corner onto our street, lugging my sacks of groceries, which somehow seemed to grow heavier with every step, when a car rolled up to the curb beside me.

"Hey, lady, need a lift?" Ruth shouted through the open window. "I'm on my way to Hazen's."

"You bet I do. That's the last time I buy a bag of

potatoes when I don't have my car," I said as I stowed my bags on the back seat.

"I really enjoyed last night," said Ruth. "It was great seeing Pieter again. I haven't seen him much over the past few months."

"I sometimes feel that way myself," I said with a wry laugh, climbing into the front seat of Ruth's New Beetle. Freely admitting that this recent purchase was motivated by fond memories of the Bug she owned as a university student, she claims that her acquisition made her an honorary boomer ("You boomers can never say no to nostalgia" is one of her favourite maxims).

"We've both been so busy with work," I continued. "And then there's all the kids' activities." I shrugged. "There just isn't much time left over for the two of us."

"You are currently in the busiest segment of your life, Meredith. These are your hectic, harried years. Why do you think we're hearing so much about the fact that our lives are out of balance?" Ruth asked.

"I don't know," I replied. "Because our lives really are out of whack?"

"Boomers' lives are suffering from extreme time deficit as they struggle to juggle jobs, kids, marriage, tend to the needs of elderly parents and squeeze in a couple of minutes for themselves. And because there are so many boomers, you set the social agenda. So that's why we're hearing so much about the time crunch these days."

"In the meantime, I'm stuck in the middle of it and feeling that my marriage is paying the price," I said.

Ruth parked in front of our house. "I know this is not much of a consolation, Meredith, but if you can ride out this hectic period of your life, you have a good chance at being happier in your marriage than you were as a newlywed." She opened her door. "Here, let me help you take your groceries into the house."

"How can you say that?" I asked, grabbing the heavy bag of potatoes.

"I was reading an American study last week. It reports that the stresses of work, kids and all the other myriad issues you're dealing with right now do serve to decrease people's satisfaction with marriage. But if those people can hang on to their marriage for over 30 years, they're likely to be happier than they were on the day they married."

I couldn't believe my ears. For the third time today, I was being advised to focus on the long term. Maybe I should start paying attention to this theme! "I've heard this message before," I said. "Keep my eye on the long run, right? Don't get bogged in the details, right?"

"Well, not quite," replied Ruth. "The small stuff is still very important in a marriage — like whose turn it is to take out the garbage — but your focus has to be long term."

"Thanks for the advice, Ruth," I said. We were indoors now and piling the bags on the kitchen counters.

"It's always easier to dole out advice than to implement it, Meredith," stated Ruth. "I'm off to Hazen's to talk about Dylan. That's the family stuff I was alluding to last night."

"Hazen was telling me Dylan's thinking about opting out of graduate school for the time being."

"I know the standard advice about keeping your

children motivated and letting your kids make their own decisions. I've heard it all. But it's tough to apply it to your own family," she said, shaking her head as she headed for the door.

"Well, don't get bogged in the details," I quipped. "Seriously, Ruth, you and Hazen have been great parents to Dylan. You'll get through this one too. Don't forget, it must be difficult for him too, having two such accomplished parents."

We stood together at the front door. Ruth impulsively hugged me and held me tight.

"Thanks for the support," she said, before turning her gaze to Hazen's home across the street.

After supper on Sunday evening, the kids settled down to finish off their homework. I decided I'd do a bit of homework of my own to get ready for my first day on the job. I headed down to the basement where Pieter and I keep our old university textbooks (thank goodness we're both such pack rats!) and pulled out an economics text I'd used in first year. I just wanted to make sure that I understood the fundamentals of saving and investment.

Saving, the text told me, occurs when a household doesn't spend all of the income it has left after paying tax — its "disposable" income. So, if a family receives more income during a year than it spends consuming things like food and clothing, that money forms its annual savings. Okay so far. Now, those savings — that "non-consumption use of the household's income," according to the text — increases the household's asset holdings. That means the family's wealth increases. Now it started to come back to me.

I remembered being confused by these concepts when I was at school. When I was a kid, saving meant going down to the Royal Bank on the corner and depositing my hard-earned babysitting money into a savings account. The amount in that account was my savings. Simple. But economists don't see it that simply. They look at personal saving as only one aspect of the savings picture. Personal saving is one part of "gross national saving," which also includes saving by corporations and governments. And an economist's definition of personal saving is broader than that of the average layperson. To an economist, personal saving includes paying off debts like a mortgage, putting money into pension plans and insurance policies, or investing in stocks, bonds and mutual funds. It's any income that isn't spent as it comes in the door on the consumption of goods or services or payment of taxes, but is set aside for the accumulation of wealth.

Wealth and personal savings are two different things. A household's net worth is its wealth. Subtract liabilities from assets and you're left with wealth. As we knew from experience, wealth can be negative as well as positive. Pieter and I had come dangerously close to having more liabilities than assets. When we lived in the suburbs, we watched the price of our house fall very close to what we'd mortgaged it for — we'd bought at $280,000 and sold for $225,000. Our wealth evaporated before our eyes. Wealth is measured at a point in time. When we sold our house, we were too close to being net debtors.

Since we'd moved to the Glebe, we'd been able to save and increase our wealth.

Savings can increase wealth in a variety of ways. Paying off a mortgage reduces liabilities, which increases wealth. Stuffing money into a mattress increases a household's wealth. Investing money in stocks and bonds adds to wealth by increasing the household's assets.

The personal savings rate — that all-important number that scares the wits out of Hazen's clients — is that percentage of disposable income that is saved. And that number is in serious decline, not only in Canada but also in the United States.

So where does investment fit into this picture of saving and wealth? People invest their savings in assets in order to increase their wealth. Financial investments can take a number of forms: the purchase of shares, bonds, real estate, GICs, even artwork. Again, economists have a different definition of investment. For them, investment means spending on capital goods, things like factories and machinery. That spending increases the ability of the economy to increase its output of goods and services — what economists call "capital formation." But it's people's personal investment — their savings — that makes capital formation possible. If a person buys stock in a company, that company will use the money to build a factory or acquire new machinery. And that's a good thing. That's what keeps the economy chugging along, our standard of living rising.

Without both savings and investment, our economy couldn't continue growing. Investment turns savings into capital goods like computer chips and airplanes, which, in turn, increase the amount our country can produce. Savings provide a source of capital for making investment possible. But the decision to save is made by individual households and is quite independent of the decision by corporations to invest. And — this is where it starts becoming confusing — savings and investment each have opposite effects on the economy. Savings — the part of our income we don't spend — decrease consumption and reduce economic demand. If you're saving your money, you're not out spending it. Investment — spending by corporations on capital goods — increases production both today and tomorrow. As a result, investment expands the economy.

If saving exceeds investment, this will not help our economy grow. In fact, that strategy would probably lead our economy headlong into a recession. When saving is greater than investment, consumption falls and that makes our economy contract. The economy relies on current consumption — the purchase of everything from cars to shoes — to keep growing. The Japanese economy gives us a good example of an economy at a standstill, where people are saving more than ever before. That money is finding its way into personal safes and across the ocean to other countries but not into the Japanese economy. And that's bad news for Japan!

But more investment than saving is not good either. That will lead to increased investment and consumer demand and, possibly, inflation. We've been down that path before, during the 1980s. Higher inflation inevitably leads to higher interest rates, investment slows, and before we know it, the economy is in a recession.

It's just like life, I thought. It's all about finding that perfect balance. With enough saving and enough investment, we end up with a healthy, sustainable economy.

"Mom, where are you?" called Emily from the top of the stairs. "I'm finished my homework. Will you read some *Swiss Family Robinson* before bed?"

"I'm down in the basement. I'll be up in a second," I replied. Reading about a family marooned on a desert island — where saving and investing were of no concern — sounded like a good diversion for what remained of a Sunday evening. I closed my old textbooks and stacked them back on the shelf. I felt ready to tackle whatever Hazen could throw my way and I'd alleviated some of my new-job jitters. Sometimes, I contemplated, it's not bad being in over your head a little.

4

wwww.savings.ca

I knocked on Hazen's door at eight-thirty on Monday morning. I was feeling very pleased with myself for reviewing my economics texts the night before.

Hazen swung the door open. "Come on in," he said, ushering me into the front hall. "I have something to show you." He led me into his study.

"This is new," I said, pointing to a chair and table I had never seen before.

"That's what I wanted to show you. I brought it down from Dylan's room. Since we'll be in here a fair bit over the next few months, we both might as well be comfortable."

"Thanks, Hazen," I replied, settling into the new chair. "So, are you going to give me my marching orders this morning?"

"I want to talk a bit about the type of information I

think I need before I set you loose on the StatsCan library," he replied. "You've heard my seminar. You know that I spend a fair bit of time talking about where I think the interest rate and the inflation rate are headed in this country, courtesy of the boomers."

"Sure. You point out that interest rates and inflation rates are likely to stay stable and low for the next decade or more."

"Right," he said. "And I think the boomers are behind the continued stability of North American interest and inflation rates. Of course, I'm assuming that no big catastrophes are looming on the horizon — a nuclear war or immense natural disaster. I'm optimistic that we'll find a cure for the Asian flu that's plaguing the Far East. If our day-to-day lives stay relatively calm and peaceful, I see a group of boomers who are going to begin focusing on preparing for retirement in a very serious way. Boomers are chipping away, paying down their mortgages. And the end of mortgage debt is going to make a big difference to boomers — mortgage debt currently outweighs consumer debt by three to one. Once those mortgages are gone, the boomers' debt picture will be significantly brighter. That means more saving, which, in turn, means a lessening of the demand for borrowed money."

"And interest rates are the price of borrowing money," I interjected. "Low demand equals low rates."

"Hey, you've got a good memory," Hazen said, laughing. "The interest rate and the inflation rate generally move in sync. So, if the interest rate stays low and stable, in all likelihood we'll see the inflation rate do the same thing. Right now, that's where our economy stands. Low interest rates, low inflation rates. And that's where the savings rate comes in. We're looking at personal savings rates that are the lowest they've been in 60 years. My audiences want to know when the boomers are going to start saving, because that saving is what is going to help keep our interest rates in check. You've seen the headlines announcing that boomers aren't saving enough, that they're dangerously optimistic about the future, that they're doomed to retire in poverty."

"Actually, Pieter and I were just talking about that on the weekend — the media has pounced on the fact that many boomers are headed towards a dismal retirement. But there's a second issue too, Hazen," I added. "How are baby boomers' savings boosting the stock market if those savings are falling?"

"Exactly. The naysayers, who see no relation between the boomers' preparations for retirement and the stellar performance of the stock market, love to point to the current low savings rate and say 'How can it be?' Your job is to answer those naysayers."

"How do you want me to address the issue?" I asked.

"I want you to tackle the issue of boomers' savings so that I can tell my audiences how boomers are saving today and what they've got planned for tomorrow. I want you to examine both the present and future situation of saving in this country. I'm going to give you *Boomernomics: The Future of Your Money in the Upcoming Generational Warfare* by Bill Sterling and Stephen Waite. The authors are global strategists with a New York firm, BEA Associates." He handed me the book together with a red file folder. I looked inside the folder to find a list of sources to check at the StatsCan library. I was on my way.

As the bus trundled west along Carling Avenue towards the library, I spent my time thinking about my upcoming summer. I still wasn't certain how things would work out with Hazen. How could I tell him anything he didn't already know? Despite my concerns, I started working through the stacks of books and articles on savings, the boomers and Canada's financial future.

In very short order, I started to learn plenty! But while my work was going great guns, it proved to be a tough week on the home front. Malcolm was his usual surly teenage self, and I received some heartbreaking news from my old friend Sharon.

Sharon and I met during Frosh Week at the University of Ottawa when a senior student selected us from a crowd, tied us together, and forced us to run a three-legged race down a gauntlet of cheering, jeering frosh. That crazy indignity served as the foundation for a friendship that continued through marriages, the birth of kids, several moves and a few career shifts. Sharon and her husband, Ron, finally settled in Guelph, where Ron, an accountant, established his own firm and Sharon found a job administering student grants and loans for the University of Guelph. We made an effort to get together with them and their two kids at least once a year — a weekend in Toronto and a jaunt to the zoo, or a visit to Winterlude and a skate on the Rideau Canal. Nothing too extravagant, but always warm and fun.

I was delighted to hear Sharon's voice when I answered the phone on Wednesday evening. My first thought was:

"Great, they're planning a trip up to Ottawa this summer." That thought was immediately dispelled.

"Meredith, I need to tell you something. Something bad." By this point, Sharon was sobbing. Her news came out in great gulps. She'd just come in from an appointment with her doctor. She'd been tired for the past few months but figured it was just the flu that the kids were passing around the house. But she became worried because she couldn't shake it. After a couple of weeks of tests, her doctors pinpointed a tumour, located just behind her right eye. Not only was it malignant, it was also inoperable. She was in for at least a summer's worth of chemotherapy and radiation. At that point in the conversation, she collapsed into tears.

Ron came on the phone. "Could you see your way clear to come down for a week in the summer?" he enquired. He'd been phoning all Sharon's friends to ask them to pitch in. They were both optimistic that Sharon could beat this thing, and he hoped that, together, we could keep her spirits up while she endured her marathon of treatments.

Still stunned, I told Ron to count on me. The kids would be out of school for the summer by the end of next week. After that, I could travel down to Guelph easily, dropping the kids at my sister's house in Scarborough. He said he'd get back to me once they'd received a schedule of the treatments. I hung up the phone and stood, stone still, staring into the backyard.

"Meredith, what are you doing?" asked Pieter, strolling into the kitchen in search of a drink of orange juice. I turned to him. Now it was my turn to dissolve into tears.

Work was my saviour that week. It seemed that until now my group of friends had been invincible. Oh, we'd had our bad luck with careers, and some were divorced, but nothing like this, nothing life-threatening. Work kept Sharon's tragedy from consuming me by focusing my mind on my research tasks in the StatsCan library. To my surprise, I was able to accomplish everything Hazen had set out for me. So it was with great anticipation that I knocked on his door early Friday morning, at the end of a week spent assembling information. I was ready to report.

"I'm looking forward to this," said Hazen, welcoming me into the house.

"So am I," I replied. "I think you're going to like what I've got planned out for you." We moved into Hazen's study. "I want to tell you about wwww.savings.ca," I continued, arranging myself into my new chair.

Hazen perked up. "You found a web site about savings in Canada? I've never seen that one before."

"Listen carefully — wwww.savings.ca," I answered.

"Oh, I get it. Four *W*s instead of three. It's not a web site at all. Okay, what's going on?" he asked.

"It took me a while to figure out how to tackle the issue of savings. I knew I needed a framework, so I divided the topic into four questions. *Why* do we save? *Where* are we now? *When* will boomer saving really get going? *What* will boomer saving mean for the future? Get it? The four *W*s," I said.

"So far, I like it. Tell me why we save."

"The short answer — we want to increase our wealth. But there's so much more to the decision. What are the motives behind the decision to save? And what affects those motives? We might want to save for retirement but lose our job or experience illness. Maybe we want to provide for a child's education, need a new car, new roof or new furnace. Or maybe we just want a vacation. Plus, different cultures feel differently about saving. For some, leaving an inheritance for children is a prime goal of saving. The possibilities are as endless as human behaviour, which can be puzzling, maddening and, very often, unexpected. In the end, despite all the differences, the vast majority of people do plan for the future. Saving is an integral part of their planning. As a result, we can distill what we know about saving to formulate theories that explain why we save."

"Let me see if I understand. You'd begin by giving a short explanation of economists' hypotheses for *why* households save. Would you then use that information to explain the *where*, *when* and *what* questions?" asked Hazen.

"Exactly," I replied. "Economic theorists have come up with many different hypotheses to explain what they call the 'savings decision.' I think it's worthwhile outlining these to your audiences because they provide a solid explanation for the boomers' recent savings habits. It's important that people understand the *why*. I know that, for me, things make more sense when I understand why things are happening — that they're not just random occurrences."

"Tell me which theories you'd present."

"The obvious one is the life cycle hypothesis. It just makes such good common sense. The patterns of life.

Everybody understands the life cycle of a household — we leave our family and maybe move on to college, university or a first job. We start out broke, borrowing money. In other words, our consumption often exceeds our income — no saving, lots of spending. If things are going right, our incomes increase with age and experience. Along the way, many of us will marry, have a couple of kids, buy a house. In a few years, we're thinking of planning for our children's educations. Before we know it, we're turning an eye to retirement. In the early years, our incomes are often not enough to cover our consumption. We're in debt. Those debts get paid as we move along and our incomes increase. Our peak saving years occur when we're between 45 and 64. There's a predictable pattern as we move through our lives. I think the permanent income hypothesis should also be mentioned."

"Enlighten me," Hazen said.

"This theory also appeals to good, old-fashioned common sense. A household usually comes to expect a certain level of income as its 'normal,' or permanent, income. This means a household comes to make its decisions to consume based on that income level. So, if that income goes up dramatically — an inheritance or, better yet, the 6/49 jackpot — that family will save more than another family for whom that high level of income is normal. Similarly, if income falls — a breadwinner is downsized out of a job, sidelined because of a serious illness or suffers a drop in income — that family will spend more than a family with the same level of income that has not experienced a change in income."

"I hope you're not going to forget the Keynesian hypothesis," Hazen interjected.

"Hold on. It's the next one on my list," I said. I chuckled silently to myself. That comment confirmed that Hazen already knew this stuff! He was just relying on me to reorganize it for him and put it into language that anybody could understand. "According to the Keynesian hypothesis, when a household's income increases, consumption also increases, but not by so much as the increase in their income."

"I've always had problems with that theory," Hazen said. "If you take it to its logical limits, for example, this theory says that savings just keep rising with a household's income level. It's not that simple. There are reasons for saving other than an increase in income."

"Right. This theory just doesn't capture all the variations in people's saving behaviour. That's why it's important to tell people that there's not one total theory of saving.

"Finally, I think you should talk about how our wealth influences our saving behaviour. So far we've been looking at the income of households and how level of income influences the saving decision. We can't forget that we don't just stuff our savings into a mattress. Our wealth generates interest, dividends, capital gains — depending on where and how we invest it. Some economists argue that as our wealth increases beyond what we had expected, we don't save as much. We don't need to save as much because we're going to reach our savings targets through our investments."

"The wealth effect," said Hazen.

"Right. The wealth effect is the economic theory that hypothesizes that consumers will spend more simply because the value of their assets has risen."

"Okay, what do you propose to do with these theories, Meredith?"

"The natural next step is to use these theories to explain *where* we are now," I replied. "The current savings rate is sitting at approximately 1 percent. Looks pretty bad, right? But I think you need to spend some time with your audience putting that number into perspective. Look at the flipside. Although our debt levels have gone up over the years, they haven't skyrocketed as many would have you believe. In fact, Canadians have very healthy balance sheets — households' ratio of debt to assets is about 20 percent. That means that for every dollar of debt, a household has five dollars in assets. That number is well within historical norms. And Canadians appear to be doing wise things with those borrowed funds. Like you were saying at the beginning of the week, the vast majority of that debt is mortgage debt, and that's being paid back in an orderly fashion. There's absolutely no evidence that Canadians have gone on a wild spending spree with stacks of credit cards. Those high-priced credit-card loans cover only one-fifth of Canadians' consumer debt. The rest is spent on pretty staid stuff — financing cars and home renovations, for example. I came across an excellent quote you might be interested in," I said, reaching into my file. "Here it is. According to the governor of the Bank of Canada, Gordon Thiessen, 'If you take the household sector as a whole, it is not buried under a mountain of debt, with high servicing costs, and no spending power.'"

"I like that," replied Hazen. "I think you're quite right. People make the automatic assumption that if savings are low then we must be getting poorer. And that's not necessarily correct. I don't think that people realize that the information the savings rate gives us is quite limited. It only provides a quick snapshot of our financial security, giving us an indication of current consumption and our current ability to save and purchase goods and services. But it doesn't tell us about our long-term ability to look after our financial needs."

"Exactly. Despite our declining savings rate, Canadians are actually getting richer. An important fact that's often overlooked is that our savings rate may have shrunk but the net worth of Canadians has increased. Our net worth reflects the assets we own and the debts we owe. While the savings rate is a snapshot, our net worth is the big picture of where we stand financially. According to some estimates, the average Canadian was over $2,000 richer in 1996 than in 1995. That's because the value of our assets has increased more than our debts. In fact, StatsCan is in the midst of surveying Canadians, calculating their wealth, in order to accurately determine their financial security. The savings rate is simply not an adequate measure of our long-term financial health. It doesn't take into account capital gains, for example. That means capital gains Canadians have earned from the increase in the value of assets like shares and real estate that is sold at a profit doesn't show up in the savings rate."

"Now you're on my territory," Hazen interjected.

"A growing number of Canadians have moved their assets into the stock market, through either the direct purchase of stocks or mutual funds. And they've reaped the benefits of the upward climb of those markets over the past few years. That asset shift is at the root of a substantial portion of the increasing wealth in this country. Just take a look at the statistics. After home ownership, the ownership of shares is the most popular investment vehicle for Canadians. There's been a massive change in the way Canadians invest. Only 15 years ago, share ownership ranked fifth in popularity on Canadians' investment agenda. Many Canadians have moved their assets, shifting them from GICs and savings accounts into the markets. And because of the health of our stock markets, those Canadians have been well rewarded over the past few years, watching their wealth increase steadily."

"That increase in our wealth certainly didn't have much to do with an increase in our incomes because, in the first half of the 1990s, Canadians' incomes fell," I said. "The average after-tax family income in this country dropped by approximately 5 percent during that time. It's only now that we're seeing incomes start to rise again, albeit slowly. And not surprisingly, the savings rate is starting to nudge upwards again. What Pieter and I experienced — dropping income, job insecurity — wasn't really that unusual, I now realize. Knowing that so many other Canadians took an economic hit doesn't make our experience any easier, though," I added wryly.

"So, now that you've set a few myths on their ears, what's next on the agenda?" Hazen asked.

"Why don't you tackle the life cycle hypothesis of saving?" I asked. "You already refer to it in your talk. Why not identify it as such?"

"We can see the marks of the boomers all over our economy," Hazen said, nodding in agreement. "Back in the early 1980s, when the big waves of boomers began hitting the labour market, finding their first jobs and setting up households, we saw interest rates skyrocket. No surprise! They were borrowing big time, buying cars, stereos, appliances and, finally, homes. That demand for money sent the price of it — the interest rate — into the stratosphere. Boomers did the same thing to the housing market in the late 1980s. Housing prices lifted off like never before. It was a great time to be selling a house, and many of your parents' generation thought they'd won the lottery as a result," explained Hazen.

"I think what many people are forgetting," I pointed out, "is that, if you take a good look at the life cycle hypothesis, the majority of baby boomers haven't yet reached their peak saving years. The serious saving years occur between 45 and 64. The median-age boomer turned 40 only in 1997. Retirement is still a long way off. And many of these boomers are still in the midst of raising their kids. That's a time for spending, not saving. Talk to any boomer parent and they'll tell you how expensive skates, swimming lessons and hockey sticks are these days! In fact, many boomer women are currently more concerned with outfitting a nursery than thinking about how they'll fund their golden years. We're seeing more older first-time mothers than ever before. Boomer women were older than their mothers when they married, and they often delayed childbearing to pursue a career. The result? Women in their thirties are giving birth to almost 20 percent of firstborns. It's no wonder the savings rate is still low."

Hazen said, "I like that example. It illustrates how expectations change over the years. Your mother expected to have children at a younger age than you did. Those life cycles change from generation to generation. We have to recognize that."

"Look at my own family. My mother was only 20 when my oldest brother was born; I was 24 when Malcolm arrived on the scene. And I was the first among my friends to have a baby!"

"This gives me an opportunity to tell how people's expectations about their incomes will affect the way they spend and save," Hazen mused.

"I'm not sure I understand where you're going with this one," I admitted.

"I can give you two good examples," he said. "Let's look at the housing market. Many baby boomers at the tail end of the generation — the Gen Xers — couldn't get into the housing market as easily as their older boomer siblings. The hard times brought about by the recession in the early 1990s forced many Gen Xers to put off buying a home. As a result, the average age of first-time buyers rose to 35 in 1997, from 32 in 1992. That recession forced an adjustment to the life cycle analysis. Now, because they got into the housing market later than their older siblings, a lot of those younger boomers are still loaded with debt. Because they're still raising kids, they're probably taking their time paying off those mortgage debts. Another reason why the savings rate is depressed." Hazen picked up a pen and jotted a note to himself.

"So what's your other example?" I asked.

"Did you read *Boomernomics*?" he asked.

I nodded.

"One of the things Sterling and Waite mention," Hazen continued, "is the change we've seen in savings patterns of retired people. Because they're financially secure — they know they can count on CPP and OAS, plus private pensions and savings — they're spending. They're the first generation to retire comfortably. In fact, they're really the first generation to retire. If you look back to your grandparents' generation, you'd find that many of them worked till they dropped. The majority of men worked until they were well into their sixties — the same age as their life expectancy. In a way, your parents' generation are retirement pioneers."

"Lucky pioneers, we should add. And, like you said earlier, we shouldn't forget the financial windfall they received when all those boomers bid up the prices of their homes."

"Exactly. And they're on a spending spree. Just look at what's happening to the cruise industry. I just read that the big cruise line Carnival is poised to build the largest luxury liner ever — the new *Queen Mary*. They're creating a new golden age of sea travel for those who missed it the first time around. But this time it's not only the aristocracy who'll be cruising across the Atlantic. It'll be a retired couple from Winnipeg with a good pension and government benefits. Those folks don't have the same incentive for saving their parents did. They feel secure — that translates into spending their loot. And our comparatively low savings rate is reflecting that now."

"My parents' generation may not have had as strong an incentive to save as we do," I said. "We're not going to have the luxury of knowing we'll be taken care of in our old age. Retirees today can count on CPP and OAS. But who knows if those programs will be around when Pieter and I retire? CPP payments to retirees are funded by today's workers. It's a pay-as-you-go plan. That works fine now, when we have many more workers than retirees. But when the boomers begin retiring, the scheme breaks down. The number of retirees will increase dramatically, with a smaller number of workers footing the bill. Today, there are about five working-age people for every senior. By 2030, there will be only three workers for each Canadian senior citizen. Think of the heights CPP premiums will hit. In *Boomernomics*, there's plenty of talk about future 'intergenerational warfare' as the bills for the boomers' benefits fall on their children and grandchildren. I agree with Sterling and Waite — those younger generations aren't going to be too keen to bear onerous tax hikes in order to fund the boomers' retirements. The government is trying to deal with the potential crisis today. CPP contribution rates will jump by more than 70 percent over the next few years in an attempt to build a CPP investment fund for the tidal wave of boomers who'll be retiring 20 to 30 years from now. Plus, the government, like individual investors, has come to the realization that the stock market is a good place to be. Paul Martin announced recently that, in order to get the best possible return on CPP funds, the government will be investing some of those funds in securities. Let me read you Martin's comments," I said, flipping through a stack of articles. "Here it is: 'CPP funds will be invested in a diversified portfolio of securities by professionals.'"

"Hmm," muttered Hazen. "The government and I seem to be on the same wavelength — a diversified portfolio and professional advice. I like it."

"Be that as it may, I don't think I'll be able to count on CPP in the same way today's retirees can. Pieter and I are not relying on receiving pensions from the government to fully fund our retirements."

"Your expectations, then, will govern your savings decisions. Because you don't feel you can count on the government, you're going to need to save more in the future. Wise move, I might add," said Hazen.

"But we're different from our parents' generation in another respect," I continued. "They could count on the ever-rising value of their home to fund, at least in part, their retirement."

"And that's one of the reasons explaining why you boomers are such financial babes in the woods," Hazen said.

I laughed. "How do you figure that one?"

"Well, your parents' big investment was a house. And that was probably the only bit of financial advice your parents ever gave you — buy as big a house as you possibly can, as soon as you're able. They never told you about bonds, stocks, money market funds. The emphasis was on real estate. What they didn't realize was that the boom cometh and the boom goeth. And the boom is gone from real estate, leaving the boomers with big mortgages and homes that have stagnated in value."

"You're right on that one," I replied. "I remember my dad proudly telling us kids that he paid $5,000 for our house back in the 1950s. By the early 1980s, that house was worth $150,000. Not a bad profit. But Pieter and I haven't had the same luck. We've lost money on our foray into the real estate market. With the boomers housed, we simply aren't going to see those big leaps in value. We can count on a house to keep the rain and snow off our heads, but we won't be able to look to our real estate to keep us financially comfortable in our golden years. That's another reason we're going to have to get going and get saving. Hey, I'm starting to sound like you, 'This time it's different.'"

"Meredith, while you're talking about changing expectations, don't forget one of the most dramatic occurrences in the financial lives of boomers," Hazen said.

"What do you mean?"

"You mentioned it earlier — the nasty kick incomes took in the early 1990s. I think that made a huge impact on a generation of boomers who believed that incomes could go only one way — up!"

"That takes you straight into the permanent income hypothesis," I said. "Boomer households expected to see their incomes go up in the 1990s. Like you said, we'd never before seen a downturn in our incomes. As a result, even though they were watching their incomes decline, the boomers kept spending, albeit at a lower rate than in the prosperous 1980s. The result? The savings rate took a serious hit along with their incomes."

"I think many boomers had a hard time during the 1990s resisting the siren call of the North American advertising machine," said Hazen. "Boomers were raised to consume — clothes, cars and convenient appliances. They feel that they deserve their stuff — and plenty of it."

"Those attitudes could account for some of the spending. But, like we said earlier, the consumer debt statistics don't show a generation gone wild with credit cards. You're giving us a bad rap we don't deserve." I laughed. "But you're directing this conversation into my next question: *when* are we going to start saving?"

"Saving has certainly hit the collective consciousness. The media is on high alert now, generating an abundance of articles questioning whether boomers will ever be prepared for retirement."

"Exactly," I said, rummaging through my files. "Here's one — 'No Improvement in Canadians' Bleak Retirement Forecast.' Well, the time is right for these articles, and the media knows the demographics of its audience. Middle-aged Canadians — the boomers — are starting to worry about where the money is going to come from to fund their retirements. Many have just begun to face the cold, hard fact that they're going to have to begin saving to ensure that those retirement years will be golden and comfortable. Listen to this quote from Angus Reid in his book *Shakedown*: 'Older people, except for those already retired on fully indexed pensions, tend to be more jittery than young people, and the big bump of baby boomers is aging quickly. Cockiness is turning into caution.'"

"I like that," said Hazen, contemplatively stroking his chin. "Well, the sheer numbers of boomers could turn us into a very cautious nation."

"Consider this statistic," I said. "A recent survey showed that those most likely to contribute the maximum to their RRSPs are aged 50 to 64. More than 40 percent of them contributed the maximum amount. But for those aged 18 to 29, that percentage falls to a mere 14 percent. Those two age groups have vastly different priorities, and those numbers prove it. But consider the power of those numbers by looking at the population projections for our country. In 1996, we had only slightly over 6 million Canadians aged 45 to 64; by 2001 that jumps to nearly 7.5 million, and by 2006 the aging boomers will have driven that number up to nearly 9 million. Think what a difference that's going to make to saving in this country! We're just beginning to see the long-term power of the savings boom. Again, we can use the example of RRSPs. The growth in retirement-oriented savings instruments, like RRSPs, has been greater than that of non-retirement instruments every year in the 1990s. Boomers have begun battening down the hatches."

"This is another example of the life cycle hypothesis," Hazen pointed out. "Boomers can begin saving in earnest because their kids are gone."

"And here are some statistics supporting that prediction," I stated. "In Canada, men's earnings hit their peak between the ages of 45 and 49. When men are between 60 and 64 their earnings equal what men in their thirties are earning. But what we need to point out is that consumption patterns have changed significantly. The older men, aged 60 to 64, likely own a house — ideally paid off by the time they're 60. Their kids are through school and have likely moved out of the family home. So, although he may have seen his income decline, that 60-year-old man has proportionally more of his income available to save than a 30-year-old with two young kids."

"Hold it. Don't forget that plenty of those 60-year-olds are watching their adult kids move back in with them." He laughed. "Look at Ruth and me. We've got a twentysomething moving back in at the end of the month."

That little comment, I thought, was a good sign. Hazen was finally starting to see the lighter side of Dylan's move back to Ottawa.

"Dylan won't put the same financial burdens on you as a young child does," I replied.

Hazen gave me a "who knows?" shrug.

"Plus," I continued, "a 60-year-old has the motivation to save: he's facing retirement straight in the face. For a 30-year-old, retirement is way off in the future."

"All of this is going to translate into good news for the stock market," said Hazen. "But you've just touched upon another message that I want to make clear to the audience. RRSP information is good news for many Canadians. But it would be even better news if Canadians preparing for retirement began earlier rather than later to consider the merits of contributing to an RRSP. Something like 20 percent of Canadians have never contributed to an RRSP and the majority contribute less than the maximum. Fill up your RRSP! I'd really love to get that message out loud and clear to anyone concerned about retirement.

The miracle of compound interest will secure a comfortable retirement."

"There's another thing that might be discouraging younger boomers from seriously preparing for retirement," I said. "I think that more than a few boomers are living in hopes of inheriting the cash that will fund their retirements."

Hazen harrumphed. "That's a fundamentally flawed approach to financial planning, akin to counting on winning a lottery. There's no doubt that boomers are poised to inherit a phenomenal amount of money over the next few decades. Estimates set the amount at an almost unimaginable $1 trillion. And that too is going to be great for markets as the boomers sell their parents' houses and other assets and shift that money into stocks and bonds. But what boomers have got to realize is that this is a general phenomenon. Boomers won't share in this pot of loot equally. In fact, many individual boomers — because their parents are particularly long-lived or encounter serious health problems requiring expensive care, or are poor to begin with — will end up empty-handed."

"You've overlooked the obvious, Hazen. Many boomers are the extremely unlucky children of those oldsters who drive recreational vehicles with bumper stickers reading, 'I'm spending my kids' inheritance.'" We laughed together.

"And more power to them," said Hazen. "Whatever the reason, I would advise the average boomer to plan for retirement without any regard to the possibility of an inheritance. And, if an inheritance does materialize, well, that's gravy."

"While we're talking about the future, I think we should talk about the last W — *what* does all of this mean for the future?" I said.

"I do like that Reid quote: 'Cockiness is turning into caution.' We're poised to become a nation of savers," replied Hazen.

"Pessimists will have a field day with that one. They don't see a golden age of saving, they see an economy lurching to its knees, mired in savings." Those naysayers point to Japan, currently mired in recession yet still sporting a healthy savings rate. In fact, the Japanese are saving more than ever. Too much saving, because this means less consumption, can crash an economy. The pessimists see that happening in Canada when the boomers begin saving in earnest."

"It's difficult to compare today's Japan with tomorrow's Canada," remarked Hazen. "While we were restructuring our economy in the 1980s and early '90s — downsizing, job-shifting and retooling — Japan continued on in the same traditional ways as it always had, with lifetime jobs and conservative business strategies. As a result, a significant portion of the hefty amount of money saved by the Japanese is sitting in personal safes rather than invested in the Japanese economy. The Japanese are now concerned about the solvency of their once-great banks. And that underlines the importance of a stable financial services sector. Solid financial institutions keep money in the market circulating for investment. We're lucky in Canada — we have those stable institutions."

"Despite the pain and dislocation it caused, our restructuring left us with a renewed, revitalized economy,"

I added. "Hazen, it's another 'this time it's different.' Unlike the Japanese, our savers are eagerly looking to invest in the businesses that power our healthy economy."

"I agree," said Hazen. "I see a future where an educated, mature Canadian workforce saves at a reasonable rate yet continues to consume. Unlike the Japanese, Canadians will not be motivated to save by fear of the future health of the economy. No, they'll be saving to provide for their retirements. But they'll still want to enjoy the journey along the way. I think we'll see a healthy balance where boomers will be able to save more than they have been in the past but still be very interested in spending to enjoy the present."

Hazen glanced down at his watch. "Meredith, it's nearly one o'clock. We've been chatting for over four hours. That was excellent work — you really covered all the bases. Listen, I have some tuna sandwiches made up. Nothing too fancy. How does lunch in the garden sound?"

"As long as somebody else is fixing lunch, sounds terrific! But, Hazen, I've given you only half of the savings picture. So far, we've only discussed personal saving. After lunch, I want to talk about gross national saving — the big saving picture that includes not only personal saving but also saving by corporations and government. That big picture, I might add, is looking pretty good." With that, my first presentation to Hazen was behind me and I breathed a huge sigh of relief.

We spent a leisurely hour chatting over sandwiches and iced tea. I spoke to Hazen about my friend Sharon, and he kindly told me that we'd arrange my work around her needs. Flexibility, he told me, is one of the beauties of being self-employed. We yakked about our kids and their foibles. Just as we were clearing up, Ruth breezed into the garden.

"I thought I might find you two back here. I'm just stopping by for a couple of seconds to arrange my social life," she announced. "Meredith, I stopped by on the off chance that we might be able to arrange lunch together some time next week."

"And I'm left out," interrupted Hazen.

"Don't fret, Hazen," chided Ruth. "I want to ask you about going to see Cirque de Soleil this fall. Dylan's never seen them and I thought we could take him for his birthday. Are you interested? I can pick up the tickets."

"I'm certainly interested in lunch next week," I said. "I'll be working at the StatsCan library. Can you pick me up there?"

"No problem. I'll call you next week to arrange the details. Hazen, how about you?"

"I'd love to see the circus. Didn't we see them about 10 years ago?"

"Yes, that was a great evening, but it was just you and me. I don't know where Dylan was back then. Perhaps Dylan is right — maybe his return will be good for the three of us." She laughed, bending to give Hazen a kiss on the cheek. "I'm off. I'll pick up the tickets on the way to the university." And with that she breezed out of Hazen's backyard.

We both stared after her. The world always seemed a bit diminished once Ruth had left. Her energy filled any place she was present.

"Ruth seems to be around more than I remember," I began, tentatively. I didn't want Hazen to think I was being nosy.

"Relationships change," he said quietly. "Marcel Proust wrote that relationships are 'as eternally fluid as the sea itself.' Ruth and I are at a particularly interesting juncture of our relationship." He stood and began clearing the lunch plates. That was as much as I was going to learn today.

Our afternoon session was as productive as its morning counterpart. We discussed national saving — the sum of private saving, both personal and corporate, and public saving.

"Public saving was a real non-starter until recently. Governments were spending, not saving," I led off. "But things have truly changed over the past few years. We're finally starting to see governments with surpluses rather than deficits. In fact, the drop in personal saving has been offset by rising government saving."

"At the federal level, the government has not only a balanced budget but a surplus to boot," remarked Hazen. "We haven't seen that happen for nearly 25 years."

"And I think boomers are the leading advocates of this turnaround. Boomers have placed reducing government deficits on their political agenda."

"And governments have been able to comply, in large

part because of low interest rates and a healthy economy," Hazen added. "I agree, however, the boomers want their governments to be fiscally responsible."

"And I have a great way for you to tell your audiences about that. I drive Malcolm out to Nepean every Saturday for a golf lesson. Near the driving range, there's a road sign that cheerfully proclaims: 'Welcome to Nepean. We're debt free.' That's the power of the boomers. Ten years ago, when boomers were busy having babies, that sign would have read: 'Welcome to Nepean. A great place to raise your children.' But times have changed, and boomers now want all levels of government to run themselves without racking up debts."

"You just watch. In 20 years, that sign is going to read 'Welcome to Nepean. A great place to retire,'" mused Hazen. "It all comes back to the power of the boom."

"The boom doesn't explain quite everything, Hazen. Like David Foot, the co-author of the demographic bible, *Boom, Bust & Echo*, says, the boom explains about two-thirds of everything. Technology has significantly transformed the national savings picture in Canada."

"Please explain," said Hazen, settling himself in his chair.

"This is part of your 'this time it's different' theme. We all know how technology has transformed our personal and professional lives. Well, it's also transformed the way our economy works. Think back. Industry used to be a big smelly affair of belching smokestacks and huge factories. Railroad, oil and chemical companies dominated the stock markets. Look at our economy now — computers, communications and health care are what we're hearing about. Just look at our own city. Twenty years ago, Ottawa was a government town — period. High-tech companies like Nortel, Newbridge and Mitel are now our big growth industries."

"'Economy lite' is the term used to refer to our new economy," said Hazen. "Peter Bernstein, the author of *Against the Gods: The Remarkable Story of Risk*, coined the expression, I believe."

"It is a lighter economy — physically lighter. We simply don't need the same kind of business investment we once did. Back in the 1920s, some 50 percent of business investment was poured into the physical plant — factories and warehouses, for example. That has been steadily declining. Today it stands at about 30 percent. The remainder is invested in equipment. And that equipment — courtesy of technology — isn't nearly as expensive as it once was. Think about how much you paid for your first cell phone. Now they're trying to give them away so long as you'll agree to a service contract. Well, the same thing has happened in the business world. The relative price of machinery and equipment is shrinking. According to research by economists with the Royal Bank, the price of investment in equipment and machinery relative to the price of all goods and services is today just over a quarter of what it was in the mid-1960s. That means more bang for each investment buck."

"And it's that investment that promotes the continued growth of our economy. But, Meredith, don't forget that there is a demographic explanation for this transformation. Back at the turn of the century when thousands of immigrants were arriving on our shores and, later, when the baby boomers were arriving on the scene, Canada was in the midst of a population explosion. The country needed massive investments in new infrastructure — homes, schools, railroads, highways — to physically support all those new people. Granted, we now need to support and maintain that infrastructure — look at all the road work that's under way in Ottawa this summer! But demographics has also played a significant hand in transforming our economy."

I laughed. "Hazen, you can introduce demographics into any and every conversation."

"Interesting you should say that, Meredith. I'd like to talk to Pieter this weekend about my thoughts about boomers and technology. I'm convinced that the rapid growth and acceptance of new technologies in our country is due, in large part, to the baby boomers."

"How do you figure that?" I asked.

"It's quite simple, actually. The boomers are better educated than any previous generation. And boomers still make up the lion's share of the workforce. Technology works in this country because the boomers have the skills and education to use that technology. If the boomers didn't have the ability to adapt to new technologies, our economy would not have transformed itself into 'economy lite,'" he concluded.

"I've been reading Louise Yamada's book, *Market Magic*, this week, and she suggests that technology is playing a role in smoothing the bumps in the business cycle. She points out that technology has made business much more efficient and cost-effective. Look at the way companies can now manage their inventories. With forecasting software, big retailers can eliminate large inventories of consumer goods that previously sat idle — and cost a bundle to finance — in warehouses. Streamlined operations like that translate into greater profitability. I predict that will keep interest rates down."

"I don't see the connection," I confessed, amazed at how Hazen could always tie his theories into such a neat package.

"New technology works in two ways," he explained. "In the example I just gave, it helps to reduce the amount of money a company needs to borrow to finance its inventory, for example. The hi-tech industry — economy lite — is simply less capital intensive than the smokestack industries. Taken together, both reduce the demand for, and therefore the cost of, money."

"While we're on the topic of the hi-tech sector, I know that Pieter is working on some interesting new Internet software that he's been wanting to discuss with you. We're around this weekend and you're welcome to drop in at any time. Could be a fruitful meeting," I said.

The remainder of our Friday afternoon was spent reviewing my notes on saving. It had been a great day, learning that I had met — maybe even surpassed — Hazen's high standards.

5

Caught in the Web

We began the weekend with a minor domestic disaster.

My first Saturday-morning task was to tackle the Mt. Everest of laundry that had built up during the week. I had just started my first load when I heard a horrible squeal from the antiquated washing machine — Pieter and I figured it was probably as old as we were — and turned just in time to see sudsy water shooting out the top, a tiny, perfect version of Old Faithful in my basement.

Hearing my shouts, Pieter ran down. Unable to fix the machine, he cursed the thing and said that if it was up to him ("If we weren't renting this damn place . . ."), we'd be heading straight to Sears to buy a new one. So, there we were standing in an inch of water, both cross, both ready to hurl the washer into the middle of the street — but we still had a couple of tons of laundry to finish.

What a great way to start a summer weekend. But then I had a brainstorm.

I packed all the laundry into green garbage bags, located Malcolm's old Radio Flyer wagon in the garage (thanking my stars once again that, pack rats that we are, we hadn't sold it at a garage sale) and headed upstairs to wake the kids.

"Five bucks for both of you if you take the laundry to the Clean Scene down by Hank's Hardware," I told them. "And you can buy anything you want for breakfast." The Clean Scene is a laundromat cum diner that's become a fixture in the Glebe. Emily and Malcolm were up in flash — bribery, used properly of course, can be an amazing tool for a parent.

Pieter and I were standing at the end of the driveway watching them towing the wagon behind them when we caught sight of Hazen rounding the corner of his house. It being Saturday morning, he was in his gardening clothes — by the end of June, his garden was already looking pretty lush.

He waved. "What are you two watching?"

We crossed the street and told him our tale of woe — a rented house, a broken-down washing machine, a landlord who didn't want to spend any money on new appliances, kids trundling laundry to the laundromat.

"Well," he said thoughtfully, "maybe it's time for the two of you to start thinking about buying a house."

"Hold it, Hazen," cried Pieter. "Last year, you told us we were clever for renting rather than buying. Make up your mind."

"Times change," replied Hazen, "and you've got to

change with them. Maybe you're ready for your own home again. I'd be glad to talk real estate with you — just name the time and place. But before we do that, I want to ask Pieter something. Meredith told me you're working on some new Internet software, and I need to speak with someone who can take me beyond all the hype that surrounds the Net. Would you tell me what's going on?"

"Me? Tell *you* something?" Peter laughed. "Hey, that's a nice change. I'd be delighted! Make me a cup of coffee and I'll sit down with you right now."

"Mind if I sit in?" I asked.

"I'm hoping you might take some notes," replied Hazen. "If you don't mind working on a Saturday . . ."

"This hardly qualifies as work," I said as we headed into Hazen's house.

I could hear the two of them chatting in the kitchen as I went into Hazen's study to search out a pen and a pad of paper.

"It's just like an enormous spiderweb," I heard Pieter saying as I returned to the kitchen. I knew he was talking about the Net because I'd heard him use the analogy before. "Let's look at the way communications have developed," Pieter continued. "The telephone let us speak to one person. The printing press lets one speak to many. In the same way, radio and television let one speak to many. But the Internet blows them all out of the water. It allows many to speak to many. It truly opens up the world. And it's opening up that world very, very quickly. It took approximately 70 years for the telephone to be used by half of the North American population. The Internet has been accessible to Canadians only in the past few years and already over 30 percent of them are surfing on their home computers. Look at e-mail. It's become the Internet's fastest-growing area."

"Why's that?" asked Hazen.

"Look at what e-mail does," explained Pieter. "It allows companies and individuals to send information in a way that's very quick and easy. And — here's the real attraction — it's cheaper than any other communications technology. This means that companies can contact their consumers directly, economically and conveniently. What more could a company ask for?"

"I'm certain they're hoping that contact will result in a sale to those consumers," Hazen said.

"Exactly," said Pieter as he watched Hazen prepare the coffee. "And that's what e-commerce is all about, what its proponents call 'business without boundaries.' Here, I'll get the mugs, cream and sugar organized and, when we sit down, I'll give you'll a little primer on the development of the Net."

After a few minutes of bustling about Hazen's kitchen, the three of us headed for Hazen's front porch with a tray loaded with coffee and cinnamon rolls.

"Okay, let's start at the beginning," Pieter said. "The Internet connects thousands of separate computer networks around the world. It began its life in the United States, linking academic, military and government agencies. But then the personal computer moved into homes and businesses throughout the world and the rest, as they say, is history. Pretty recent history too. The Internet only began its move outside academic and government circles in the early 1990s."

"That makes perfect sense," remarked Hazen. "That's when the PC revolution took hold. Back in 1986, only 10 percent of households had computers. By the mid-1990s, that figure had grown to approximately 30 percent."

"And the introduction of the World Wide Web, that spiderweb collection of computers that lets those users easily navigate the Net, has meant that the Internet is accessible to anyone," stated Pieter. "Emily and Malcolm use it all the time for school projects or to correspond with friends. I'll give you an example. Emily couldn't find her checkerboard the other day. She was moaning about it, so I suggested she check out the Web. Within a couple of minutes, she'd found a site where she could play interactive checkers. Then, she wanted to play with me, so we printed off a checkerboard and had a couple of games. I'm sorry to say she beat the pants off me." We laughed.

"But this is what I find fascinating about the Net," said Hazen. "Let's look at your story about checkers. Why would you ever go out and buy a new checkerboard when you can simply print one off the Net for free?"

"You've hit the nail on the head with that comment," said Pieter. "That's what is really different about the Net."

"Aha," cried Hazen. "This time it's different!"

"It *is* different," said Pieter seriously. "The Net is poised to shake things up. I'm convinced that we'll someday recognize the Net as a bigger phenomenon than the printing press."

"So, you're a true believer in all the ballyhoo that surrounds this new technology?" inquired Hazen.

"No. I'm not denying that there's been a lot of unsupportable hype around the Net. Like any revolutionary technology, the Internet has brought the snake oil salesmen out of the woodwork. The hype has always got ahead of what the Net can actually do at any given time. If you listen to the hype now, you'd think everybody was buying whatever they'd like, whenever, over the Net. Well, e-commerce is not there yet.

"But let's focus on what the Net can do in the future," continued Pieter. "Before the printing press, the only people who had books were a minuscule segment of the population who could feed the monks who produced books by hand. The printing press changed the way knowledge was disseminated. It paved the way for universal education. Similarly, the Net allows for almost universal access to much of the information that currently exists in the world. It's already proven itself a research tool extraordinaire. It's truly changed the way academics work. Globalization is a given. Conservative estimates place the number of Net users around the world at over 50 million — some claim 90 million people are exchanging information over the Net. By 2000, that number will explode to well over one billion. StatsCan tells us that, in 1990, Internet access tallied 2 percent of Canadians. By 1995, 17 percent were cruising the Net. As I said earlier, that number has now blossomed to well over 30 percent."

"Boy, you sound like me, reeling off those statistics," said Hazen as he poured our coffee.

"Well, the Net is a big part of my business," answered Pieter. "And I'd wager it's going to be a big part of nearly everyone's business in the future. In fact, some 400,000 businesses now have a web site — open for business."

"What projects do you have in the pipeline?" asked Hazen. The two of them were really into this now. I enjoyed watching them together. It must be a hormonal thing — like watching two guys settle in at a barbecue or a hockey game. Part of their secret club, the ancient order of males.

"Everything that we're working on revolves around e-commerce," Pieter explained, "buying and selling goods and services over the Internet. We're developing software that allows companies to mine the Internet for information. It will collect information from people who are surfing the Net, compile that information and send it on to companies who can then relay customized information and advertising to those Net surfers."

"Can you give me an example of a practical application?" asked Hazen.

"Okay. Let's say our customer is a large hotel chain. We can give a Net surfer a review of that hotel chain's web site. And, when the surfer checks the review, we can enquire as to the vacations she's just taken and where she's planning to go next. We could even ask what newspapers and magazines she likes to see in her hotel room, for example. Let's say we find out that she wants to visit Vancouver and she reads the *National Post*. We compile that information and pass it along to our customer, the hotel chain. The chain then contacts the surfer directly and informs her that they can offer her a special rate in their hotel in Vancouver and that they'll deliver a complimentary copy of the *Post* every day she stays with them."

"Very clever," replied Hazen. "And very boomer friendly. This fits perfectly with the boomers' desperate bid to carve out more time for themselves. Somebody will do the legwork for you — for free!"

"That's a big part of this new technology — saving time and, as a result, making business more efficient and, therefore, more profitable. It's a pretty simple equation: simplify, save time, make money," said Pieter. "Boeing is a company that's often cited as being on the cutting edge of this wired world. As you can imagine, aircraft manufacture requires millions of parts. Many of these parts come from contractors who supply Boeing. Keeping track of all these bits was a logistical nightmare until the Net surfaced. The web connects Boeing and all of its suppliers, allowing every member in the chain to know where each part is along the supply pipeline. It's efficient, it's fast and it saves a ton of money. Boeing expects the savings to tally in the millions of dollars and it also expects that, within a couple of years, it will be doing all of its business over the web. And Boeing has a warning for suppliers who aren't already on the web: if they're not on, they won't be doing business with Boeing. That's the power of the web!"

"It's certainly an example of how the marketplace will be changing over the next few years," Hazen commented.

"It's really all about changing valuations. We're going to see the value — and the way we calculate the value — of goods, services and businesses change radically," replied Pieter.

"How do you mean?" asked Hazen.

"Well, let's look at the travel industry. The Internet is

going to be a very serious threat to the way travel agents work today. Why do you need a travel agent when you can get travel information from around the world and make reservations, instantly, in your own home? The Net is going to change the value of airline tickets, for example. Let's say you want to go to Vancouver or Venezuela or Vienna. You're short of time, as boomers are wont to be, so you probably just call Air Canada and take what you can get. In the future, you're going to post your travel itinerary on the web and place the ball in the court of the airlines that fly to those destinations. Which airline can come back to you with the best price? There are already services on the web that auction off tickets. You enter your destination, dates of travel and the price you want to pay. They come back to you with your tickets!"

Hazen laughed. "Competition does have a way of reducing prices."

"And the Net does have a way of making certain businesses obsolete. What do you think is going to happen to the travel agent who has a little storefront in your neighbourhood mall?" asked Pieter. "This is a good example of the way values are going to change in the future. That travel agency is not going to be worth much in the coming years. But there's more. Look at the big picture. E-commerce is in its infancy today. The total global e-commerce market totals about $13 billion. By 2002, experts expect that number to hit nearly $450 billion. That's a lot of value. The Net is going to change the way we buy and sell goods and services. Consumers, courtesy of the web search, are becoming a very knowledgeable bunch. Car buyers, for example, can now go to the web and find out all about the profit margins of the dealers. Now, that bit of information gives them a solid edge when negotiating a price for their new wheels. And look at a company like eBay. It's put a completely new spin on the term 'flea market' by providing vendors with an electronic stall — for a fee, of course. According to the company, over 700,000 auctions take place at its site every day. You should take a look at the site — computers, cars, toys. It's a shopper's paradise, bringing together buyers and sellers who had no hope of meeting before this technological bazaar was created back in 1995."

"The Internet is definitely going to change the way we value companies that employ the Net effectively — and those that don't," agreed Hazen. "A company like eBay bases its considerable value squarely on the Net. Other companies just run more efficiently because of technology. Your example of the hotel chain is a good one. If that hotel chain can increase its occupancy rate through the Internet, then that's ultimately going to make the company more profitable and more valuable to its owners, the shareholders. But the Internet is going to blow the companies that are still producing old-fashioned checkerboards right out of the water."

"Hazen," I interjected, "maybe you could use changing valuations as a result of the Internet as an analogy in your talk."

"What do you have in mind, Meredith?" he asked.

"Well, the Internet creates new businesses, renders many others redundant and changes the valuations of all sorts of things we thought could never change. Ten years ago, who would have thought travel agents could be rendered obsolete? Isn't that like the stock market? Think of all the analysts and commentators out there who are screaming that stocks are currently overvalued. Maybe — just maybe — the rules of the game have changed. Just as the Internet will transform the economy, maybe the stock market is in a period of transformation. Maybe the way stocks are valued is changing."

"That's good, Meredith. But let's not forget to bring the boomers into the discussion. I'd like to talk about the way the boomers are driving the economy, focusing on the multiplier effect of technological innovations. All forms of computer technology can be employed in North America because of their easy acceptance by the well-educated boomers and the generations that come after them. Taken together, we're witnessing a revolution."

"I think you make a good point about North American acceptance of new technology," said Pieter. "And that's what's going to keep this continent out front in the global economic foot race. There's a new book out by Robert Kaplan, *An Empire Wilderness*. He writes that our history has always been driven by technological change — nothing is permanent. We're good at adapting to changing, evolving circumstances."

"See, 'this time it's different' with the proviso that 'it's always different.'" Hazen chuckled.

"Here's what's really different," answered Pieter. "The media hype surrounding the Net makes it sound as if it's dominated by cyberpunks, young adults and teens. That's just not correct. A recent U.S. survey of Internet users showed that more than half are baby boomers in their thirties and forties. Yes, younger users are more likely to socialize online, using chat rooms and e-mail. But, listening to what the two of you have to say about the boomer time crunch, I'd hazard a guess that's because young people have more time on their hands than the boomers who are actually using the Net purposefully. Interestingly, older Net users are like the younger users. They use the Net for socializing. With the kids out of the house, they've got the time too."

Hazen laughed. "Pieter, this conversation has confirmed my beliefs about the Internet. In the future, we'll all be heading to the electronic mall."

"So, does that mean you'll be advising your audiences to invest in Internet stocks?" I asked.

"Not so fast," he answered. "Internet stocks have been on a pretty wild ride recently. Every time I open the newspaper, I see that Amazon.com or Excite or Lycos or Yahoo! has hit a new high. Companies that were only a spark in some computer nerd's imagination a couple of years ago are now worth millions more than businesses that have been around for decades. Yes, lots of people are going to make a lot of money with Internet stocks. But with that wild ride comes risk. This is a market that is in its infancy. It needs to sort itself out."

"What do you mean by that?" I asked.

"I'll give you one example that represents thousands of similar events in the technology arena. You've heard of iStar?"

"We use iStar," I replied. "It's a company that provides Internet access, connecting subscribers to the Net. It's Canadian, isn't it?"

"iStar was a Canadian stock market darling when it

first went public. On the first day it traded on the TSE, it leapt from $12 a share to $22. It's tempting to jump in and get on the profit bandwagon." Hazen stopped, balancing his coffee cup on the arm of his chair. "Particularly tempting for baby boomers who've only seen the stock market climb ever upwards. But that would have been a big mistake for the long-term investor. Eventually iStar was bought by PSINet for under a dollar a share. Big gains but big losses too!"

"That's the way this business works," commented Pieter, wryly. "Hi-tech is risky."

"Let's look back — new technologies are always risky investments. There used to be over 100 automakers in Michigan at one time. The market matured and 97 of those firms don't exist any longer. Now it's just the Big Three — Ford, Chrysler and GM. The same thing is going to happen with the technology market. There's no doubt that these new technologies are becoming an incredibly significant part of our economy, and it's natural that these technology companies should become major players on our stock exchanges. But, as you can see, the odds of choosing the winner in the battle of the Internet companies today are pretty long. Tons of money is being poured into developing new technologies — high-capacity networks, for example. But we're not going to see the payoff of all that investment for a few years. That contributes to the risks of this market. At this juncture, picking the big winners of the future is simply guess-work. Right now, Internet stocks are a market for traders, not investors. You've heard me talk about my philosophy of long-term investing?"

"Right — focus on good, solid companies that you can love forever," I replied. "That eliminates a lot of hi-tech startups."

"I'm going to change the subject completely," said Hazen. "I have something for the two of you." He went into the house and emerged with a newspaper clipping in his hand. "Did you see this? It's all about the workings of the teenage brain. I thought it might alleviate some of your concerns about Malcolm."

"I didn't see this," I said, taking the proffered clipping. "What does it say?"

"The teenager's brain," Hazen explained, "works differently from that of an adult. Evidently, teenagers process emotions more intensely than adults and it's likely they don't always understand what we're telling them. It's all related to the chemistry of the brain."

"Aha, Malcolm has an excuse!" said Pieter, laughing.

"Actually, things have been more settled with Malcolm lately. I think we're calling in our chips, in a way," I told Hazen. "Pieter and I always spent a lot of time talking with both Malcolm and Emily when they were younger. Now, unlike many of his friends, Malcolm will still talk with his parents. Force of habit, I guess. But it's served our family well. We've had a couple of good chats recently about the importance of mutual respect in our family. I know we haven't seen the end of his teenage antics, but things are better. Thanks for the article, though. I had a gut feeling Malcolm's brain was different from mine," I said, impressed by Hazen's concern for the dynamics of our household.

"Speaking of kids," said Pieter, "when's Dylan coming home?"

"Within the next couple of weeks. He's driving up with a friend and they're stopping to see some sights along the way. He should be here just after Canada Day," said Hazen. "And you know, I'm like you, Meredith. I think I've finally come to terms with him. I think it will be good for him to take a year off. I'm looking forward to doing some family things. Dylan's talked Ruth and me into travelling down to Stratford with him to see some plays this summer. It'll be like old times, he says."

"In a changing world of computers and the Internet, the old times can be pretty comforting," I said, collecting the coffee mugs and placing them back on the tray. "We should get home and tackle the mess in the basement."

"Hold it," replied Pieter. "Hazen hasn't upheld his end of the bargain. He promised to tell us why we should think about buying a house."

"I'm around all day tomorrow," said Hazen. "I want to talk about more than real estate. I also want to pick up the theme you raised today, Meredith."

"What was that?" I asked.

"Changing valuations. But not the changes caused by the Internet. I want to talk about changing stock valuations."

"Okay, it's a deal," replied Pieter, hoisting the tray and taking it away into Hazen's kitchen.

6

Headcounts Count

"Look," I said as Hazen swung open his front door in response to my knocking. "Look! I bought this copy of *Vanity Fair* just for you. I want you to look at this advertisement. I've never seen anything like it before!" I turned to a page filled by a photograph of a beautiful woman modelling lingerie. What made this advertisement so special? The beautiful woman was at least 50 years old, her face, though still luminous, lined with tiny wrinkles, the battle scars life awards its survivors.

"Hmm," said Hazen, flipping through the magazine. "I assume you're surprised because the typical lingerie ad features a fit, young 20-year-old."

"I guess I am a bit surprised, but mostly I'm delighted to see that the advertising industry is finally waking up to the fact that they're selling to people like me. And we're not 20-year-olds any more. Quite frankly, I want to see how lingerie will look on *my* body, not that of some half-starved teenage model," I replied. "And she looks pretty good, if I do say so myself!"

"This ad really does make good sense in the context of this magazine," said Hazen. "Here's an article on the health care system — a growing concern of all aging boomers. Here's another on a boomer pop-music icon, David Bowie. This magazine's target market is you! Welcome to the future. Say goodbye to those teenage, waif-like supermodels!" We both laughed.

"I think you should mention this in your seminar," I said. "This is visual evidence that the world is changing — literally, growing older."

"I just might," Hazen replied. "What I really like about this ad is its tag line." He flipped back to the lingerie ad. "'There comes a time in life when finally (how long has it taken?) you are simply true to yourself.'"

"It captures the contentment that can come with maturity — if you're lucky," I said.

"I'm convinced that you make your luck, Meredith," Hazen said evenly. "To quote the scientist Louis Pasteur, 'Chance favours the prepared mind.' In fact, this is exactly what I want to talk to you and Pieter about today. Are you around?"

"It's such a gorgeous day," I said, gesturing at the brilliant blue sky, "that we thought we'd take the kids over to Gatineau Park for a picnic lunch. You could join us if you'd like."

"A picnic," he replied slowly. "I haven't been on a picnic in years. Sounds good. I can go over to the bakery on Bank Street and pick up dessert."

We finalized our arrangements and I trotted home to dig our picnic hamper out of the basement.

The kids ran ahead and found us a picnic table.

"Here, Mom." Emily waved, pointing at the table, as Pieter, Hazen and I strolled across one of the meadows dotting the grounds of Kingsmere, the estate of Canada's longest-serving prime minister, William Lyon Mackenzie King. He may have been a bit loony — conducting seances with his dead mother and all — but his purchase of these 600 acres in the Gatineau was inspired, particularly now that the estate is open to the public.

As Pieter unpacked the picnic hamper, the kids started throwing a Frisbee around. Soon a friendly black Lab pup had joined in their game.

"See," said Hazen, pointing at the dog, "another retriever. You boomers are nuts about your pets. I read a recent survey of pet owners that revealed that if these people were stranded on a desert island, more than half would prefer to be there with their pet rather than another human."

"That's crazy," stated Pieter. "Who conducts these surveys, anyway?"

"I hope you like egg salad sandwiches, Hazen," I said.

"One of my favourites. I'm contributing an apple tart to the feast." He placed a bakery box on the picnic table. "But before we get started on our lunch, I was wondering whether you wanted to talk about real estate."

"Great!" said Pieter. "I want to hear what's changed your mind on the subject."

"Nothing's changed, actually," Hazen answered. "I'm convinced that real estate is no longer the investment vehicle it was back in the 1970s and '80s, when the boomers were in the midst of housing themselves. And you know what happens to prices when demand outstrips supply! Your parents reaped the financial rewards of selling their homes to this gigantic group of buyers. But things are different now. The boomers are housed and the surge of buyers is over. The smaller baby bust generation can't continue the home-buying bonanza. The larger echo boom generation won't be buying homes until the 2010s. And even that's not going to amount to a real estate boom because so many boomers will be wanting to move out of their family homes at that time. We'll have a situation where we'll see lots of demand but an equal amount of, or maybe even more, supply as boomers downsize."

"So are you saying that housing was overvalued in the '70s and '80s?" I asked.

"Not at all. Those astronomical values were justified back then. People were willing to pay those prices. They were overvalued compared to today's market. But that comparison is completely theoretical. And hindsight is always 20/20. I'm not buying a house today in the 1980s market. When we're valuing any commodity — housing, food, stocks — we've got to look at the here and now. What's it worth today? Then, when we're determining whether that commodity is going to be overvalued by tomorrow's standards, we've got to factor in our best guess, based on a combination of historical evidence and future predictions and estimates. And I'll tell you right now, there is nobody who can accurately predict what lies ahead. The result? There are many, many times in our lives when we have to stare into the future and throw the dice," said Hazen.

"So, this is what it boils down to — pure speculation?" asked Pieter.

"No. Ideally the guesses you make — whether it's a decision to buy a home or invest in a stock — will be educated guesses. That's one of the reasons we're talking about valuations today. Part of that decision making is an attempt to figure out whether the commodity you buy will hold and, you hope, increase in value in the future. But there are some basic facts we can't overlook. If I'm the only guy selling water in the desert, I can charge a lot more than the fellow selling water in downtown Ottawa. The price of the water in the desert is overvalued compared with the water in Ottawa. But if you desperately need a drink in the desert, that's a minor detail. And, as we mentioned during our discussion of the Internet, values and the way they're calculated do change, depending on where you are and when you're there."

"So what's going on now?" Pieter asked. "I keep reading about how hot the real estate market is — housing starts are up in nearly every large community."

"That, I believe, is a result of pent-up demand. Now that the economy is healthier than it has been in the past five or six years, those people who put off buying a home have entered the housing market, giving it a temporary injection of life," explained Hazen. "In the long run, real estate looks dismal as a place to invest money.

The better way to look at a home is a place to live. There's a journalist in the U.S., Craig Karpel, who says that we have unreal expectations of the values of our homes. He says that we don't go to a restaurant, eat a delicious meal and then leave, expecting the owner to pay us. Why, he asks, should we have all the benefits of living in a house and expect to be paid for the privilege of enjoying that experience? Many experts predict that if boomers hang on to their real estate too long, they'll see some of their equity vanish. I think that many people are beginning to understand this. Large numbers of folks have seen their monthly mortgage payments decrease in the face of falling interest rates — either they've renegotiated their mortgages or their mortgages have come due. In any event, we haven't seen these people out there buying bigger and better houses as a result. No, many are staying put, realizing that the biggest house they can afford to carry may not be the best investment."

"Well, that's not good news," I said. "So why on earth are you suggesting that we should get back into the market?"

"Let us live while we live," replied Hazen, with a grin on his face.

"What do you mean by that?" asked Pieter.

"We should strive to live for today and plan for tomorrow," replied Hazen. "I guess what I'm really saying is, don't live in either extreme. I see people who have never saved a dime and live only for the moment. Others save everything they can get their hands on and live like paupers today. Take my word for it, neither extreme is good for the soul and, looking at the big picture, neither is good for the economy. We should be doing some of each — a little saving, a little spending . . ."

"I don't know," muttered Pieter. "We very nearly lost our shirts on our first foray into real estate."

"So that's it?" A slightly sarcastic tone had entered Hazen's voice. "You're not going to have what you want because you're afraid to take a chance? Life's not going to be a very fulfilling experience if you don't take some risks along the way."

"Risk is a big part of my work life, Hazen," replied Pieter. "I'm not so sure that I want to have risk become a significant element of my personal life too."

"I'm not talking about gambling here," Hazen said with a chuckle. "The real estate market is like any other. You research, you study, you assess the risks you're facing — and then you go for it. I know both of you — you'll regret it if you choose the cautious course. Let's take a good, hard look at the real risks here." He paused, staring in turn at both of us, ensuring that he had our attention. "Some things have changed for the two of you over the past year. Pieter, you in particular seem to be having some serious issues about living in a rented home. Look at your reaction to the washing-machine imbroglio. You're not happy. I think it's time to ask yourself whether, for your own peace of mind, you should start looking around for a home to buy. Your business has picked up, Pieter, and the financial plan you put in place last year is already paying dividends. Maybe the time is right."

"But how do we avoid the mess we got ourselves into last time?" I asked.

"I think if you pay close attention to the market, you

can minimize that kind of risk. First and foremost, pay attention to demographics. That means stay away from starter homes out in the suburbs. There's nobody to buy them now. Second, adhere to the golden rule: Buy what you need and not what you think you want. In other words, be realistic about your needs and your pocketbook. A local magazine recently published an article listing the 500 most expensive homes in Ottawa. Well, I know a few of the people on that list who are using way too much of their income to support that fancy house. It's so important for them to be in the right neighbourhood that they're willing to risk their future security — they don't have enough income left over after paying the mortgage to save for the future. That's just dumb! Third, be very careful about the location and neighbourhood you choose. Your best bet would be a neighbourhood that serves as large a community as possible. By that I mean you want to be in an area that appeals to all ages. For example, many suburbs cater only to families with young kids. By looking for a neighbourhood that appeals to a broad cross-section of the population, you'll increase the number of potential buyers when you go to sell."

"It all boils down to supply and demand," I said. "Where do we find these mass-appeal neighbourhoods?"

"You're living in one right now," replied Hazen. "Walk along the streets in the Glebe and you'll see all ages and all varieties of households. That's because the neighbourhood is very central, close to downtown but with great parks and shopping and services within walking distance. The Glebe is an example of a neighbourhood where housing is going to hold its value. There! I've given you my best guess on the valuation level of real estate in the Glebe."

"But we could get more house if we bought out in the burbs," said Pieter. "We'd easily pay $225,000 for a 1,500-square-foot house in the Glebe. We could get 3,000 feet way out in Orleans for that money. I just don't know. I do know that I'd love to be in my own home."

"Those are the trade-offs. Life's full of them," replied Hazen.

The kids came running towards the picnic table. The Frisbee, they told us, was stuck way out of reach in a pine tree. Did we want to come watch them as they climbed the tree to retrieve it?

"What's a picnic without some high drama?" said Hazen as we followed the kids towards a grove of pines. "And what's life without some risk?"

After polishing off our sandwiches and demolishing Hazen's apple tart, I asked the kids if they would walk up to the tea room to buy the adults some coffee. After a few moans and groans they took off. Despite their protests, I was pleasantly surprised by the family dynamics of the day. Emily and Malcolm were actually getting along. Giving them a focus — preparing the picnic lunch, playing Frisbee, fetching coffee, anything! — seemed to reduce their desire to bug one another. And, out of the house, Malcolm had reverted to his pre-teen cheerful self. Maybe, I concluded, we should do more of these family outings. The family that plays together stays together, as my dad used to say.

Hazen had just returned to the table after taking a load of paper plates to the garbage bin. "I wonder," he began, "if you wouldn't mind being my guinea pigs this afternoon. I'd like to get your comments on something I'm thinking of including in my new seminar."

"I can't think of a better way to spend a lazy Sunday afternoon," I said. "Tell us what you've got on your mind."

"We've already touched on the subject twice in our recent conversations. It concerns valuations. But this time I want to talk about stock valuations. As you mentioned yesterday, Meredith, plenty of commentators are screaming that stock prices are overvalued. And that's one of the questions I hear at my seminars: 'Aren't these high stock prices a sign that the market is a very risky place to be?'"

"You've got to admit that it's natural to become nervous when a good thing like the current bull market goes on for a long time and prices appear to be launched into the stratosphere," Pieter said. "Maybe people are just natural pessimists — what goes up must come down."

"I think that's part of it," commented Hazen. "But what I'd like to do in my seminar is start out with the basics — much like you did with your work on the savings rate, Meredith. When these commentators talk about overvaluation, they're usually focusing on two ratios that have traditionally been used to measure the health of specific stocks and the market in general: the price-earnings ratio and the dividend yield."

"I'm assuming you'll explain those terms for the audience," I said.

"Yes," replied Hazen. "At its most fundamental, stock

valuations are all about the future well-being of a company. How much will it pay out in dividends? What will its earnings be in the future? Stock valuation is one of the ways experts value the future worth of a company. PE ratios and dividend yields are indicators that experts use as signposts directing them to what lies ahead. As with any sign, however, it must be read correctly. The price-earnings ratio is calculated by dividing the price of a company's stock by its earnings per share. Let's look at an example. If a share is selling for $30 on the TSE and it generated earnings of $3 per share, then its PE ratio would be 10. This means that an investor is willing to pay $10 for the ownership of $1 of the company's earnings. Generally, a high PE ratio means that investors are optimistic about the future success of the company — they see a bright profit picture ahead. High profits in the future translate into high future dividends and earnings. People are willing to pay for that through higher current stock prices."

"Okay — that's pretty straightforward," said Pieter. "How about a definition of dividend yield?"

"The dividend yield is another ratio," began Hazen. "This one is calculated by dividing a company's latest annualized dividend — the cash a company pays out to its shareholders — by the current price of the share. It is generally accepted that, all things being equal, a higher dividend yield represents greater value and a more secure investment."

"So why do many commentators think the current PE ratio and dividend yield are so out of control?" I asked. "And the next logical question is: *Are* they out of control?"

"Let's start with the PE ratio," Hazen said. "As recently as 1995, the PE ratio on the TSE 300 was around 17 times earnings. Historically, the market's PE has floated between 15 and 20 times earnings. Right now it sits at slightly over 30. It's a natural conclusion that this is too high. Natural — but not necessarily correct. Today's PE ratio has to be examined in today's context. Too many commentators are looking at it in yesteryear's context."

"So what's changed?" I asked.

"What many commentators overlook is that the PE level rises as inflation falls," stated Hazen. "In the early 1960s, for example, when inflation hovered between 2 and 3 percent, the TSE 300 PE averaged about 18 times earnings. By the 1970s, however, when the Canadian economy was mired in inflationary times, the TSE averaged about 8 times. This inverse relationship is easy to explain: when inflation is high, interest rates are usually high. Investors generally prefer the security of safe-and-sound GICs to the rough and tumble of the stock market when interest rates are high. But guess what! Both inflation and interest rates are sitting at the lowest levels they've been at in decades."

"And the boomers are at the root of it all," interjected Pieter. "Because of the boomers — their need to save for their future, their desires to see the government pay down its debts — we're likely going to see low inflation and interest rates continuing on into the future. That could explain higher-than-average PE ratios."

"That's a key part of the equation," agreed Hazen. "But don't forget to factor in the twin forces of technology and globalization. We've seen profound changes in the world of business over the past few years. Who could have conceived of a company like Microsoft 30 years ago or that Nortel would be selling phone networks to the Chinese? I know that, in the short term, many foreign countries don't look like great places to invest. But, looking long term, the future growth potential of the companies investing in these countries is enormous. Companies like these — with healthy rates of earnings growth — generally command higher PE ratios than those that have a lower growth rate in earnings."

"So, are you saying that we should ignore the old rules concerning PE ratios?" asked Pieter.

"No." Hazen shook his head slowly. "On an individual basis, stocks that have PE ratios that are way above the rest of the market are generally not the best investments. That's a sign that purchasers have enormously high hopes for that stock. Be assured that if it doesn't perform, they'll ditch it — pronto! And I'm certainly not saying that we're going to see a situation where PE ratios are going to progress in a straight line upward. Boomers will doubtlessly see plenty of corrections along the road to retirement when the PE ratios of the stocks in their portfolio will fall. But — and I hate to sound like a broken record here — I'm not surprised to see higher-than-average PE ratios these days. And my best guess is this trend will continue. North American stock markets have become very attractive places to be for investors from around the world too. Foreign investors see stable companies that are run in the interest of the shareholders — companies that aim to deliver the highest possible returns for their shareholders. Experts like economist Peter Drucker point out that in many foreign countries, maximizing shareholder value is not a valid corporate goal. As a result, billions of foreign dollars flow into our North American stocks. Investors, led by the boomers, are coming to the realization that the spot for the best returns on their investments is the stock market, despite its many gyrations. Stocks in North American companies have become a very sought-after commodity. Higher valuations are the result."

"What about the dividend yield?" I asked. "You said that a higher dividend yield makes for a more secure investment."

"That's the traditional way of thinking," replied Hazen. "The old rule of thumb stated definitively that stockholders should sell when the yield drops below 3 percent. Today it sits at 1.5 percent for the TSE 300. Selling at 3 percent would have taken investors out of the market five years ago. By mindlessly adhering to the old rules, investors would have missed the TSE doubling in value over that time."

"What's changed so radically to alter that rule?" I asked.

"Fundamental to a high dividend yield is the payment by the company of cash dividends to its stockholders. If there are no or very low dividend payouts, then there's automatically a lower yield than if there's a generous dividend. What many people overlook is the fact that paying a healthy dividend is not the only sign of a prosperous company. In fact, many very prosperous companies are going to become healthier by paying no dividends at all — for the time being," stated Hazen emphatically.

"How do you figure that one?" said Pieter.

"Do you take home every last penny that your company earns?" asked Hazen.

Pieter smiled. "The government takes plenty of those pennies in taxes before I can even get my hands on them. Seriously, though, a significant portion of our earnings are reinvested in the company — buying new equipment, for example. You have to keep up to date in the hi-tech world."

"You're not alone. Plenty of companies choose to defer the payment of dividends today in order to reinvest that money in the company with the hope of paying out even greater dividends in the future. Other companies choose to buy back their own shares rather than paying dividends. These companies — poised for robust growth — show very low or no dividend yields. Stick to the dividend yield rule and you'd miss out on these companies."

"So you're saying we should ignore the old valuation rules?" I asked.

"The old rules are helpful but the signs they give must be read in today's context, today's economy. In the first half of 1998, our economy boasted a GDP growth of over 3 percent, leading the G7 countries, but our inflation rate is under 2 percent! Typically, with growth comes higher inflation and higher interest rates. That nasty combination of high inflation and interest rates cripples growth. A vicious circle. But now we've got growth with low inflation and interest rates. It's unprecedented and it bodes well for Canada's investment climate. The stock market looks like a very good place to be — for many, it's the only place to be given the flat real estate market and low interest rates. And that demand drives stock prices up. So, the old valuation rules need to be interpreted within this environment and tempered by our view of the future."

"What about the 'new' economy we hear about all the time? Is that having any effect on changing the way we look at valuations?" I asked.

"Definitely. The new economy — based more on technology, consumer-product and service companies — is proving less volatile than its predecessor, an economy based on manufacturing and natural resources. So what does that mean for stock prices? It translates into more predictable earnings, and that means less risk and higher prices. But there's more. The new economy stocks — companies like Microsoft and Nortel, for example — have really seen their prices run up in the past couple of years. Nortel, for example, has a current PE of over 30 times. JDS Fitel, another Ottawa hi-tech company, has a PE of nearly 35 times. The PE ratios of companies like them has had the effect of skewing the entire market. Many stocks of more traditional companies have more traditional PE ratios. Look at BCE Inc. — another fine Canadian company — with a current PE of just over 20 times."

"Do all these mergers have an effect on stock prices?" I asked. "The big news recently was the merger between two Canadian entertainment businesses, Alliance and Atlantis. But the proposed Canadian bank mergers have been hot news too."

"Yes, merger mania has played a significant role in making things different this time." Hazen chuckled, proud — I could tell — at working in his pet theme. "The deals, both in Canada and the U.S., have been big ones, particularly those in the financial industry. Experts suggest that the resulting mega-companies will produce better profit growth than they would have individually. So that's driving up stock prices. But there's also the fact that when the market knows a merger is afoot, that sends stock prices higher than they would normally be, thus altering valuations."

"Hazen, you hardly touched on your favourite subject, the baby boomers. What are demographics doing to valuations?" Pieter asked.

"We can credit the boomers for raising valuations a couple of different ways. Companies are benefiting enormously from boomer employees — they're well educated and they're currently at the peak of their productive years. That's great for the profitability of those companies. But we can't forget the buying power of the boomers — and they're aiming it straight at the stock market. Back in 1983, share ownership was the fifth most popular investment vehicle for adults in Canada, way behind Canada Savings Bonds, home ownership and GICs. Today, share ownership is ahead of every other investment vehicle besides owning a home. That's a profound shift," explained Hazen.

"Yet another difference," said Pieter with a smile.

The kids suddenly re-emerged from the forest path, carrying Styrofoam cups of steaming coffee for us.

"Thanks, guys! Hey, you two sure took your time," I said.

"Yeah, we stopped in to see Mackenzie King's cottage," Emily said. "The guide gave us a little tour. We were the only ones there."

"It was kind of neat to see where a prime minister slept," added Malcolm. "The guide showed us his bedroom and where his dog slept too. While you're drinking your coffee, can Emily and I take the path over there?" he said, pointing to a small sign at the edge of the forest.

"That's a great idea," said Pieter. "The three of us are right in the middle of a discussion. Do you have your watches on?" The kids both nodded. "So, be back here in 30 minutes. If you're not back by then, we'll send out a search party." With that they headed off.

"I can't believe how well they're getting along today," I mused, watching them run for the path.

"Here's the thing," began Hazen. "Their relationship is very much like the current valuations of the stock market."

Pieter laughed. "I can't wait to hear this explanation."

"Is this newfound relationship a short-term thing or will it be around for the long term? Will Malcolm and Emily be fighting like cats and dogs tomorrow or will they be taking ski vacations with their own families when they're both in their thirties? It's the same question that needs to be posed about the stock market. There have been several major shifts that affect the way we must think about the stock market. When we see shifts like this, we must decide whether they're short-term phenomena or if what we're seeing constitutes a fundamental long-term change."

"So, how do you know the difference?" asked Pieter.

"My opinion is that we must look at the big picture," replied Hazen. "And the big picture looks pretty good these days. As a result, I think the things that are driving the change in the way we look at valuations are here to stay for a good long time. We're in a period of global peace. Granted, there are hot spots in the world — the Middle East is always a serious issue — but generally we're in a peaceful interlude of our collective history."

"There might be peace," I said, "but what about all the news we're hearing about the sorry state of the economies of many foreign countries? Look at all the problems Russia is facing. That's got to have an effect in our global marketplace. I've heard commentators predicting a global recession."

"There's no doubt that the world's financial markets are interconnected in a way they weren't in the past," said Hazen, nodding. "First, I think we should keep this in perspective. Russia accounts for about 1 percent of the world's economy. But the collapse of Russia's economy can't be ignored. And I think the woes that Russia is experiencing will serve as a wake-up call for the global capitalist system. It's in the world's interest to support that system. The North American economies are at the centre of the system and we're made stronger if the countries at the periphery — Russia, Brazil and Indonesia, for example — are healthy. We're already seeing calls from international experts like financier George Soros to support financial authorities in the international arena, including the World Bank and the International Monetary Fund. I'm very hopeful."

"What about looking a little closer to home," said Pieter.

"You mean the domestic scene," said Hazen. "Well, look at how our governments are cleaning up their finances. By reducing their reliance on deficit financing, they've made this country a more appealing place to invest. Finally, the markets are functioning extremely efficiently. Back in the 1980s, we saw stock scandal after stock scandal in the U.S. Today's North American markets have done an admirable job of policing themselves. That breeds confidence. And confidence affects valuations."

"That makes good sense," I said. "But you know that you're always going to have the old-timers who say things just don't change."

"Well, I could certainly point out some fundamental shifts that have occurred in the past," suggested Hazen. "We want to learn from history, not get stuck in it."

"What do you have in mind?" I asked.

"Until 1958, for example, stocks always offered a higher yield — the annual return on an investment — than bonds. Bonds were thought of as a higher-quality investment — less risk — than stocks, so bonds didn't offer as high a yield as stocks. And then in 1958, it all changed. Yields on stocks dipped below bonds. Many commentators predicted disaster for the markets, pointing out that just before the crash of 1929, stock dividend yields fell to the level of bond yields. Of course, there would have been traditionalists back in 1958 who were fearful when this happened. Those folks probably pulled their money out of the stock market and plunked it in bonds. Well, they'd still be in bonds because that old indicator — bond yields should always remain higher than stock yields — fell. And it's never gone back."

"What happened to make things different?" I asked.

"Commentators like Jeremy Siegel have suggested that chronic postwar inflation changed the way investors judged the yields on stocks and bonds. He points out that the benchmarks for valuation hold only so long as the underpinnings of the economy don't change. And we're seeing changes now. Just like those today who are pointing to the higher-than-average PE ratios — calling these an unequivocal signal to get out of the market. They're waiting for the old rules to kick back in. I'm suggesting that they might be waiting for many, many years." Hazen paused. "If investors had been guided by historical averages and decided to stay out of the market because the average TSE 300 PE ratio was higher than, let's say, 16 times, they would have missed most of the 1990s, when PE ratios sat at over 20 times for most of the decade."

"Boy, they would have missed a lot of good years in the market," said Pieter.

"Every once in a while a new way of thinking comes along. Because of a shift in society or technology, whatever, we're just not going back to the old ways of doing things. There's a book written by Robert Gardiner entitled *The Dean Witter Guide to Personal Investing*. Gardiner is the former chairman of Dean Witter. In his book, he points out a very practical change in the way the stock market works. Back in 1967, the New York Stock Exchange shut down on Wednesdays. On all other business days, it closed at 2 p.m. The reason?" Hazen asked, smiling.

We both shrugged and shook our heads.

"Volume!" Hazen shouted, pointing skyward. "The market was inundated. They couldn't handle the number of orders from investors. What was the volume that was shutting the markets down? Thirteen million shares. Amazing, isn't it? Today technology has made the market available to everyone. We have access and we also have the technological capacity to handle all comers. On one day in October 1997, the markets were off 500 points, and the volume, for the first time, exceeded one billion shares in a single day. This is a great example of how technology and the boomers can work together to be extraordinarily powerful," Hazen extolled.

"That's a big difference," I added.

"Yes. It was different in a couple of ways. First, the volumes are now huge — approximately 100 million shares each day on the TSE and about 600 million shares on the NYSE. Technology has allowed this to take place. But it's also different when you look at who is now in the market. In the 1950s, rich people traded stock with other rich people — no RRSPs, very few mutual funds, no giant pension funds investing huge amounts of money. There wasn't a place for the small individual investor. Now, the market has opened up, and this translates into more volume. It's different now because the average person is in the market. Technology aided this movement but, ultimately, these folks are in the market because they have to be. The average investor needs to plan for retirement. John Q. Public is showing up in the markets," concluded Hazen with a flourish.

"Yes, but if you live by the old rules, we should be fearful of that fact," said Pieter.

"Wasn't it Joseph Kennedy who said that he decided to sell his stocks in the late 1920s when his shoeshine boy started giving him stock tips?" I said.

Hazen chuckled. "I'd remind you that Joseph Kennedy also coined the expression 'Don't get mad, get even.' And part of getting even is avoiding the noise and looking at the big picture. There are plenty of differences between the shoeshine boy of 1929 and 1998. Back in the '20s, it was all about speculation, quick in and out of the market, buying on margin, short selling. Yes, that still occurs today, but the average investor is like you. Someone who's looking to fund their retirement, looking to stay in the market for the long run. Today, the shoeshine boys are investors for the long run, not speculators for the short term."

"And that's where we come in. I never thought I'd be an investor, with my savings invested in the stock markets," I said, sipping the last drop of my coffee.

"You're the person who needs to know that despite all the things that are different, there are some fundamentals that are the same as they've always been," remarked Hazen.

"Aha, you're admitting that it's not different!" accused Pieter.

"*Plus ça change, plus c'est la même chose*," tossed off Hazen. "Much of what we hear about valuations should be of interest only to the short-term shareholder, the one for whom investor sentiment is crucial to their stock market decisions. They are concerned with investor sentiment — what other investors will pay for their shares. They're not necessarily looking at the long-term picture of health and growth potential of the company whose shares they hold. Today's investor sentiment can be ignored by the long-term investor."

"I'll bet you're back to your 'buy stocks you love and hold them forever' theme," said Pieter.

"Right. And that's what is not different. Long-term investing is always about patience. My 'round rocks' theory."

"Round rocks," I said. "Sounds interesting — are you going to tell us about this one?"

"Nope," said Hazen, picking up his empty coffee cup. "I'm saving it for us to work on tomorrow, Meredith. You'll just have to wait. It looks like everybody's finished their coffee. Why don't we exercise more than our jaws. Let's head down the path and see if we can find the kids."

7

Round Rocks

"We're going on a field trip this morning," said Hazen as he welcomed me into his house Monday morning.

"But I've got some research work to do at StatsCan concerning global demographics," I replied.

"It can wait until tomorrow. Today we're working on the round rocks theory. Have you heard me speak about my friend Francis Wallace?" he asked.

"Yes, I think I have," I said slowly, trying to recall the details. "He's an older gentleman. He lives in the neighbourhood. They're over on Fourth Avenue, right? You give him investment advice from time to time."

"That's the fellow. He turned 95 last month. His wife — she's a young 93 — threw him a great birthday bash. His three kids were there — all of them in their early seventies. They're an amazing family. So, do you have your walking shoes on? We've only got a couple of blocks to go. Frank and Jean are expecting us."

"While we're strolling over, I want to know what this field trip is all about," I said. "This is a most unorthodox job. I guess that's what I love about it."

Hazen locked his front door and we set off down the street at a fast pace.

"It's very simple actually," he told me. "When I'm lecturing, people love to point to the stock market crash of 1929 and the Great Depression that followed it and suggest that scenario could occur again. Of course, I always point out that we live in a very different world now — markets are far more regulated than they were back in the 1920s, with the central banks and governments taking a far more active role in the economy than the laissez-faire attitude of institutions back in the '20s, and businesses are far more accountable now than they were back then, for example. But I'd like to give them a real example of someone who lived through the Depression — saw the stock market crash, and also saw the power of stocks to survive a market shakeup. That's where Frank comes in," said Hazen.

"Right," I said slowly, doing a quick calculation. "If Frank's 95, he would have been in his mid-twenties when the markets crashed."

"He's one of the few people left with a personal knowledge of that time. I'm going to let him tell you his story. But, before we get there, I will say that he continues to hold his entire investment portfolio in stocks," Hazen said, turning to smile at me.

"At 95! That's crazy. Don't most people shift ever-larger

portions of their assets into fixed income investments, like bonds or GICs, as they age?"

"The vast majority do. Frank is definitely the exception to the rule. But he has his reasons. For most people, this shift probably is a good strategy because they need the psychological security that moving their assets into fixed income investments provides. Asset allocation mix — the types of products that you have in your investment portfolio — depends on where you are in your life and your tolerance for risk. In today's market, an expert might recommend an asset mix of 50 percent equities, 35 percent bonds and 15 percent cash for a conservative investor. But that would vary given the investor's age. If he had a good tolerance for risk, a younger investor might want to increase the proportion of stock. Of course, asset mix also reflects the state of the markets. In unsettled markets, a conservative, older investor might reduce his percentage of equity holdings. A younger investor who sees spending many more years in the markets might want to increase her proportion of equities in a search for some stock bargains. My best answer — it all depends! Finding the mix that's right for you is very personal, and my advice would be that any investor should discuss the mix with an investment adviser," explained Hazen. By the time he finished his mini-lecture on the ideal asset mix, we had arrived at the door of a small red-brick Glebe home distinguished by a traditional centre-hall plan decorated with pretty white shutters. Hazen rang the bell.

Behind the door, we heard a deep voice call: "Hold your horses, Hazen." In a minute the door swung open to reveal a hale and hearty gentleman who didn't look a day over 85.

"I'm Frank," he said, enveloping my hand in a firm, strong handshake. "You must be Meredith. Hazen's told me all about you. Come in, you two," he said, ushering us into the small front hall. "Jean, come on down, dear," he shouted up the stairs. "We have visitors."

"Be there in a moment," came a voice from the reaches of the second floor.

"Come in and make yourself comfortable," said Frank, stepping into the living room and gesturing to a comfortable collection of overstuffed chairs.

"We've come to hear the 'Investment World According to Frank Wallace,'" began Hazen, lowering himself into a particularly cozy-looking chair.

"As you know, Hazen, there's not much to tell," said Frank with a laugh. "I've only ever invested in blue-chip stocks and," he continued, gesturing at his home, "they've provided well for Jean and me. We're still in our home and I haven't worked since 1968."

"Would you mind telling Meredith your story, Frank?" Hazen asked. I could tell from his deferential tone that he possessed a great deal of admiration for the elegant gentleman seated across from us.

"Of course. I'd be delighted. I was born here in Ottawa in 1903, Meredith. When the stock market crash occurred in 1929, I was a young man of 26. I was working in a bank. That was a very dark time in our history. The history books only capture a small slice of the grief the crash caused. Times were so different back then. The market was a speculative place. The wild times of the

1920s — the Jazz Age, they called it — caused many people to throw caution to the wind. And they did just that, buying stock on margin. That means that instead of buying stocks with money you have in hand, they would purchase them with a bit of cash down and the rest on credit. That works marvellously well when the market is going up, up, up but not so great when the markets tumble, as they began to do in early 1929, though the Black Thursday didn't arrive until October 24. When they couldn't cover their investment, many individuals and businesses lost everything. They simply couldn't repay their loans for stocks they had purchased and — this was such a difficult part of my job — the bank was forced to foreclose on them. As a result, the bank ended up with many of the stocks that they had posted as collateral for these loans. The bank took the decision that, instead of selling these stocks — which had lost significant value in the crash — they'd hold on to them.

"Now here's the interesting part of the story, Meredith. The value of just about every security we held came back, to the best of my recollection. Some stocks took a little longer than others, but by the end of the 1930s, many had recovered the value they had prior to the dramatic runup in 1929. And, of course, the rest is history. Since the '30s, stocks have posted impressive gains over the long run. What people don't realize is that many other investment vehicles saw a slide in their values in the Depression too. It's always stocks that you hear about. Well, my dear, that experience taught me a simple but very important lesson. Patience!" Frank sat back in his chair.

At that moment, his wife entered the room. It was immediately obvious that she was not in the same good health as her husband. She walked slowly with a cane but, like Frank's, her face was alive with intelligence.

"Meredith," she said, offering me her hand, "I'm delighted to meet you. I hope my husband hasn't been boring you with the stories of his stock market successes."

"Not at all," I replied. "Please join us."

"Actually, I was out at the Parkdale Market this morning and I picked up a couple of flats of strawberries. I'm just about to make a batch of my famous jam. My great-grandchildren love the stuff."

"They're not the only ones — I love it too," said Frank, watching her make her way to the kitchen. "As a result of my experience during the Depression, I developed patience and a great respect for blue-chip stocks. Over the years, I made a reasonable salary and I saved and invested in the stock market — nothing too glamorous, banks, utilities, good, reliable stuff. I started with the shares of the bank I worked for and then diversified as time went on. I always kept it simple. I went for brand names and dividends — there were no mutual funds back in the days when I started our savings plan. Many people believe that the market is too risky for them. But, over the long haul, that's simply not true. Let me show you the real risk," he said, reaching for a magazine on the coffee table. "The VON comes in for Jean each day and one of the nurses left a copy of this magazine here. It's called *People*. I'd never seen it before. The stories are quite lurid. I think they should rename it *Peephole*!" The three of us laughed.

"And," Frank continued, "who on earth is this young lad Leonardo DiCaprio, and what do all these young girls see in him anyway? It's all beyond me! Okay, here's what I was looking for," he said, holding up the magazine with a flourish. "Here's the real risk!"

We were looking at a simple ad for *Money* magazine that read: "Life expectancy in 1928: 55. In 1998: 82."

"Those are U.S. figures, but they're very similar in Canada," said Hazen. "And here's a bit of a surprise: life expectancy for men, in contrast to the past, is now increasing more rapidly than that of women."

"I'm living proof of the risk of outliving your money," stated Frank. "I must admit I'm a bit surprised to still be alive and very grateful to be in good health. Jean and I have both lived long, healthy lives and, courtesy of the long upward trend of the stock market, we're still very financially comfortable, thank you very much. My wife and I always had this one simple goal: to live out our days in this house and not be a burden on our children. Now, as you get older, you start to need assistance — the VON comes in and we also have a woman who does the cleaning — and that all costs money. I was confident of the long-term viability of securities. I'd witnessed this first-hand. I knew that was the way to fulfill our simple goal. It's a nice stroke of luck to live a long, healthy life and to see the marvels of the world unfold, but you've got to be able to afford it."

Hazen said, "Yes, that's one of the things I say in my seminar. There are two major risks in life. One is living too long. The other is not living long enough."

"Exactly," replied Frank. "That's it in a nutshell."

"You can plan for those risks," said Hazen. "A savings plan handles one and life insurance deals with the other."

"My savings plan of choice was the stock market." Frank chuckled. "Here, Meredith. You take this magazine." He handed me the copy of *People*. "I've been to Hazen's seminars. Sometimes he uses visual aids. He might want to reproduce that advertisement to show all you baby boomers what lies ahead. You know, some of our grandchildren are boomers. I think we've taught them well. They're all investors in the market. I've spent time talking with them about the importance of planning for the future.

"In fact, when each of my grandchildren turned 25, I gave them a gift: I paid for an afternoon with a financial planner. Not very exciting to a 25-year-old, but when they're my age they'll thank me for it. I want them to know how important it is to start saving early and regularly. Let's say you want to have an annual retirement income equal to $50,000 in today's dollars; start saving at 20 and you'll only have to put aside one-third the amount annually that you'd have to save if you started at age 30, one-ninth what you'd have to scratch together if you started at 50. Makes good sense to start early, doesn't it?"

"That's what Hazen keeps telling my husband and me," I replied.

"I hope you're paying attention to him," said Frank with a laugh. "I know I do. I think many young people don't save because they haven't given any thought to what lies ahead for them. And their retirement years will be very different from mine. I'm very fortunate to have a defined-benefit pension plan from my former employer, which guarantees me a monthly retirement benefit. The security of that pension allows me to take some risks with my investment portfolio — like keeping it invested 100 percent in equities. Pensions like mine are becoming a thing of the past, though. If employees are lucky enough to have a pension — only about 40 percent of Canadian workers are enrolled in a company pension plan — many are now covered by defined-contribution plans, in which both employers and employees contribute but the employee is responsible for the fund's performance. Keep that money invested in GICs for the next 40 years and you run the very real risk of not having enough money to last for what could be a very long retirement. Look at the *People* advertisement!"

"Because of the boomers, we're not going to see the government pensions we once did, either," said Hazen. "That's another thing that makes it all the more important for people to take responsibility for their retirements."

"Yes, I was telling Jean the other day that I think the government is very clever. They're planning all these changes to CPP. Younger workers will be putting more money into a plan for a government pension that will likely end up paying them less than they'd get from a private retirement savings plan. Then there's Old Age Security benefits that start at 65. Those payments are reduced for those with income over a certain level. There's certainly no free lunch!" said Frank.

"Since I'm the one who could benefit from these plans, I don't see that the goverment is that clever," I muttered.

"The cleverness comes in the fact that they've figured out — ahead of time — the impact the horde of boomers will have on these plans. Currently, Old Age Security and the Guaranteed Income Supplement account for about one-fifth of the federal government's program spending. There are fewer than four million Canadians over the age of 65 now. Think what that figure will be when all you boomers hit retirement age!" stated Frank.

"I suppose nearly 10 million boomers, including me, could make that number jump pretty high, pretty quickly. And there isn't a big generation behind us who are willing to shell out for our retirements," I said, shaking my head.

"That's where the real cleverness comes in. The government's got this all figured out and they know that, unlike you, many boomers haven't given it a thought. That's why the government is making all these pension plan changes now. The vast majority of boomers haven't focused on how the changes will reduce their government pensions. Smart to make changes before you run out of money. And start to make changes when those they affect aren't paying attention!" Frank laughed.

"It will be a rude awakening for those who haven't prepared," said Hazen. "That's why I spend so much time encouraging my audiences to start thinking about retirement. Analysts say that some 25 percent of Canadians will have less than $100,000 in savings by the time they hit retirement age. I hope I can get some Canadians worried enough to start squirrelling away more than that!"

"And then it's just a matter of patience," commented Frank, standing and walking over to the fireplace. "Here's what it's all about," he said, gesturing to the mantelpiece full of round rocks. Round rocks! I shot a look in Hazen's direction and met his steady, serene gaze.

"Frank, do you by any chance have a theory of round rocks?" I asked.

"Actually it's more of an analogy," he replied. "But it's a wonderful geological tale that my grandchildren have loved to hear over the years. And it has a direct application to investing in the stock markets. Here." He handed Hazen and me each a rock — beautiful symmetrical spheres of rosy stone flecked with shiny specks of quartz. "Jean and I collected these over the years during our hikes around Ottawa. The pinkish hue is a mineral called feldspar. All of them were once part of boulders that fell off the Canadian Shield and ended up in rivers. The current transported them downstream. It was that bouncing, rolling, sliding process that rounded off the jagged edges of the boulders," Frank said, rolling a rock around in his hands. "The farther they travelled, the rounder they became. And because these rocks, containing both feldspar and quartz, are hard rocks, that process probably took a few millennia. If you go into the bush during spring runoff, you can actually hear these boulders crashing down the riverbeds. In the autumn, when the water level is lower, the rocks move along a lot slower. But, despite the haphazard nature of the process, they still end up round. You just need to have some patience."

"Pretty simple, isn't it?" said Hazen.

"Of course, the comparison to the stock markets is an obvious one," said Frank, replacing his rock on the mantel and returning to his chair. "If you can wait. If you can endure the inevitable bounces, rolls and slides that the market dishes out, you'll end up with something pretty good. There are times when the market will move quickly, others when it will move at a slower pace. Bear markets tend to last a year or two, whereas bull markets, thankfully, can go on for several years. But the process is not a straight line. Investors must realize this and develop the requisite patience they need to watch their investment develop and grow — round off, so to speak."

"What a lovely analogy," I said.

"Well, you've been a very attentive audience, Meredith. Please, take that rock home with you as a little souvenir."

"Oh, I couldn't," I said.

"Meredith, we've got dozens of them in the garage. Over our very long lives, Jean and I have made hundreds of excursions into the bush, picking up rocks every time. They're all over the place. Just like you boomers." He laughed. "Oh, by the way, Hazen, did you know that we're planning on selling our home? We'll have to find a new storage space for all those round rocks."

"No, when did this come about?" his friend asked, obviously concerned.

"It's nothing too serious. It's Jean's arthritis. She's having a great deal of difficulty with the stairs these days, so we think it would be best to move into an apartment, where everything would be on a single floor. There are a couple of lovely old buildings a block or two from the house. We're just waiting for a vacancy. Luckily, we're both still in such good health otherwise that we're in no rush. We have the luxury of waiting for the perfect apartment. It's going to make it difficult to sell the house, however, since we don't know when we're leaving. As a result, we haven't listed it yet."

"I'm delighted to hear you're staying in the neighbourhood," said Hazen. "I'd miss our evening strolls along Bank Street. And I actually don't think you're going to have much trouble selling this home. It's in a great location and it's one of the smaller houses on the street — great potential for possible renovations. Some baby boomer couple would love to get their hands on this place! Well, Frank, Meredith and I have to get back to work. Would you mind if I just said goodbye to Jean?" He walked through to the kitchen and I could hear them chatting quietly.

We said our goodbyes at the door and began our quick march back to Hazen's house.

"That was positively fascinating. What a charming couple," I said.

"Yes, Frank is the real-life embodiment of Jeremy Siegel's book *Stocks for the Long Run*," said Hazen.

"I learned a couple of other interesting things too," I mentioned as we turned back onto Bank Street. "Did you take a good look at the cover of this *People*? It included the perfect boomer article. Look! 'Cybill Shepherd Talks Frankly about Menopause.' I love it. Even former supermodels are aging! Welcome to the boom!"

"What other interesting things did you learn?" asked Hazen.

"That Frank and Jean will be selling their home. I think

Pieter and I might be interested in looking into it. We had quite a long discussion about buying in the Glebe after our picnic yesterday. And that house looks like it would be in our budget. It's smallish and it's not at all renovated. The kids wouldn't have to change schools. It has potential," I said.

"I wondered if that house might tempt you," replied Hazen. "The long arm of coincidence, as playwright Haddon Chambers called it. It's amazing to me how things have a way of fitting together."

"Hazen, don't get the cart before the horse. I haven't yet spoken with Pieter." While he unlocked his door, I glanced at my watch. Ten-thirty — plenty of time for a quick trip to the library.

8

Reconnecting

"I'm pooped," I said with a yawn as I climbed into Ruth's Beetle. She had called me in the morning to arrange our lunch. We'd decided that she'd pick me up and we'd head to Ottawa Bagel, a couple of blocks away from the StatsCan library. "I think I need a nap rather than lunch."

"What's your problem?" asked Ruth. "You're usually full of energy."

"Crows," I replied simply.

"Crows?" Ruth said, pulling away from the curb and heading up Holland Avenue.

"A family of crows has taken up residence in the maple tree beside our bedroom. The second the sun comes up, they start cawing their heads off. That's about five in the morning these days," I moaned.

"That's a bit early to be waking up," agreed Ruth.

"No kidding! All those early mornings have taken their toll on me. And they've been particularly frantic for the past few mornings. One of the fledglings left the nest too early. It hasn't yet figured out how to fly. Its parents are unbelievably devoted, cawing incessantly, scaring away cats, swooping down on dogs, while waiting for this tiny member of the family to fly. They're pesky and noisy and now I'm exhausted, but you've got to admire the way this family of crows has hung together, protecting the smallest member of the clan."

"Most people hate crows," replied Ruth. "But I think they're the neatest birds going. When I was young, our family had a cottage in the country and one of our neighbours — a farmer — had a pet crow. It could mimic our voices and, believe it or not, it could count to four. Shiny was its name. The farmer called it that because it would steal any shiny object it could find. I hadn't thought about that bird for years," she said with a smile, edging the Beetle around the corner onto Wellington Street. "Crows are smart birds, wily and clever. They know there's power in numbers, the benefits of community. They have a complex social organization, congregating in groups that sometimes number in the thousands."

"I certainly hope we don't get that many of them in our backyard. I'll never catch up on my beauty rest." We both laughed. Ruth nosed the car into a parking spot in front of the bagel shop.

"Don't worry, Meredith — a bagel and a good strong espresso will perk you right up. You know, your crow story relates to what I'm working on right now."

"What's that?" I asked. Ruth's work was invariably

intriguing, always applicable to what was going on around us.

"Let's get our lunch," she said, gesturing to the line of customers awaiting their bagels. "And then I'll tell you."

"The need for community," began Ruth when we settled in at our lunch table. "I'm working on our need to be part of a community. The crows are devoted to their community. But we humans have been a bit careless about the way we organize ourselves. And now we're paying the price — social dislocation, isolation and loneliness are just three of the costs of our devotion to the individual over the community."

"What are you focusing on with this work?" I asked. Having worked with Ruth, I knew her articles always had their source in one idea, one concept, one comment on which she would elaborate, creating an intriguing essay.

"'All real living is meeting,'" she replied simply. "Martin Buber wrote it. Do you know who he is?"

I'd never heard of him.

"My uncle Jack introduced me to his work years ago. Buber was a Jewish religious philosopher. Born in Vienna, he died in Israel in 1965. His life's work supported the contention that we all need human connections. So, all *real* living is meeting," she explained.

"But this isn't necessarily the way the world works today. There's so much emphasis on the individual and the rights and privacy of that individual. It's as if everyone lives in their own self-contained world," I replied.

"Individualism forms the basis of North American culture. Make no mistake," said Ruth. "Our culture values the rugged loner, the brave pioneer, the strong, silent hero. My contention — building on Buber — is that by turning our backs on our need for human connections, we've missed out on the richness and benefits of community. And, as boomers age, they're searching for the missing pieces of their lives. Many of them, I'd suggest, are missing the emotional refuge that a true community provides."

"So, what are we doing about it? Are we now creating communities?" I asked.

"That's what I'm going to explore in my essay. I'm working on the notion that the need to connect is what's behind talk radio, Internet chat rooms and television talk shows. Here, let me read you some of my notes," she said, rummaging through her purse and pulling out a black notebook. "Talk radio has blossomed over the past 15 years or so. Back in 1983, there were only 53 talk-radio stations in the U.S. Now you'll find more than a thousand. Oprah was the first in the television talk-show field. And she's been followed by a host of pretenders to her throne — many of them sensationally repugnant."

"So much of that is trash TV," I replied. "My mother ran off with my husband's transsexual brother. Real garbage."

"Junk culture," agreed Meredith. "But programs like that fulfill two functions. They entertain with their outrageousness. More important, they offer vicarious connections to other people. Here's how Michael Harrison — he's an expert on the talk-media industry — sums it up," said Ruth, looking at her notebook. "'People don't know their neighbours any more, and they wouldn't have time to talk over the backyard fence even if they did. But there's still a human need for community, so it's a virtual, electronic, global media community.'"

"But they're not real connections. There's no interaction. The people watching or listening to these shows don't *really* know the people they're watching or listening to," I argued.

"You've hit the nail on the head, Meredith. Experts have called this phenomenon the 'illusion of community,' where people attempt to meet their fundamental needs for community through fantasy — in this case, an unreal media-created world. Look at the mass mournings we've seen over the past couple of years. When Diana died, when Linda McCartney died, the way some people grieved, you'd think they'd lost a close member of their family. These people couldn't or wouldn't deal with the reality that these were media events — the connections were not personal, not intimate. It's sort of like eating a Twinkie — tastes good for a minute but ultimately unsatisfying and none too nutritious."

"You mentioned that boomers, in particular, are now interested in establishing real community ties. How are they doing that?" I asked.

"I plan on using a couple of examples in this piece," she began. "First, I want to talk about Perth, the small town that's an hour west of Ottawa. *Canadian Living* recently named it as the best place to retire in Canada. Yes, Perth has low costs of living, good health care services and low crime rates, all of which are incredibly important to retirees. But what really distinguishes this place is its sense of community. You can see it in their advertising. Here," she said, flipping the pages of her notebook. "'It's small-town living at its very best . . . It's a community — neighbours, friends and families.' The town has spent a bundle on developing a thriving arts community, including a new theatre and a quaint, beautifully restored downtown. And people love the place. Nearly 45 percent of the town's inhabitants are over 45. Plenty of Ottawans retire there to enjoy this sense of belonging to a place and its community."

"It's a lovely place," I said. "I can see its appeal to people who are looking to retire in a comfortable spot."

"But it's not just retirees who are looking for community. The boomers are in hot pursuit too. You can see it in the way they're taking their vacations these days. And more than a few companies are cashing in on that desire to connect," explained Ruth.

"What examples do you have?" I asked.

"Take a look at Intrawest and Disney," Ruth replied. "Intrawest calls itself a ski resort developer, but the company is really all about real estate and building tiny, perfect villages at the base of its ski hills. We've got an ideal example only a couple of hours away at Mont Tremblant."

"We were there during March break last year," I said. "And you're right about the community thing. Intrawest had all sorts of neat outdoor activities that encouraged families to get involved. It was a fun way to meet some new people."

"If you want a real communal vacation, check out what Disney is up to these days. Have you heard about the *Disney Magic*? You can hardly miss it — it's as long as three football fields and as wide as an eight-lane highway. And here's the kicker — this cruise ship can carry 2,400 passengers, most of whom will be boomers and their kids. They're lured on board by games rooms, theme parties — all the sorts of things that bring people together. Canadians seem to be hungry for these communal trips. The number of Canadians taking cruises rose by 25 percent between 1996 and 1997."

"Funny, isn't it, how cruises used to be the domain of shuffleboard-playing retirees?" I mused.

"Times change," said Ruth. "People's needs and wants change. I'll probably include something on the renewed interest in spirituality too."

"But the statistics show that church attendance is down, down, down," I commented.

"Yet there's a huge interest in the topic of spirituality, which I think has a lot to do with our search for meaning in our lives," answered Ruth. "Where do we fit in? I came across an interesting statistic about a religious studies course offered at Queen's University. It's one of the hottest courses on campus this year — they had to turn away some 600 applicants. People are definitely thinking about religion. And family values tend to go hand in hand with religion."

"Speaking of family values, when do you expect Dylan?"

"He's driving back with a friend so he's not quite certain, but he expects to be home next week. It's funny how things happen in clusters. Here I am working on an article about the need for community and I receive a letter this morning from my own son voicing his concerns about how the members of our family are going their separate ways. He's worried that without him around Hazen and I will drift apart. In fact, Dylan's return home has brought Hazen and me together — we've spent a lot of time talking about Dylan and his issues. I guess it's natural to think that once your kids go off to university, you're finished parenting. But it's like my uncle Jack always says, 'The problems only grow bigger as the child grows.'"

"Hazen was saying the same things," I said.

"In his letter, Dylan quoted the American essayist Judith Viorst: 'Being a separate self is a most glorious, most lonely proposition . . . Separateness is sweet but connection with someone outside ourself is surely sweeter.' You know, I'm actually going to enjoy having that kid around for a while. Frankly, I don't think a year off university ever hurt anyone. He's a smart kid, he'll get back into it. He just needs a breather," she concluded.

"I sometimes wonder if we're doing our kids a favour by pushing them along," I mused.

"What do you mean?"

"Well, I look at my own kids — I expect them to do well at school and then, on top of that, to perform on the athletic field, play an instrument, learn a language, dance, sing, swim, skate and ski. It makes me wonder whether we're slathering the pressure on a bit too thick."

"You're not the first one to contemplate this question," Ruth said. "It's no surprise, really, that boomers are pressuring their kids. Boomers are better educated than their parents and boomers know that, to get ahead in this wired world, their kids need to be even better educated. It's another 'this time it's different' theme for Hazen. And boomer parents can apply that pressure because, unlike their parents, who had four or five kids, the average boomer has only two kids. Boomers can concentrate their efforts on their two little darlings. There's an interesting study of college freshmen at U.S. institutions that's been done every year since 1966. Back in the 1970s, about 20 percent of freshmen cited parental pressure as a very important reason for going to college. By the '90s, that number had leapt to approximately 35 percent."

"I see that in my own family. We talk a lot about where the kids will be going to university, what they'll be studying, careers they might choose. And we're still years away from sending a kid to university," I replied. "My kids are out of school for the summer and, I've got to admit, I'm wondering whether I should give them a leg up for next year by enrolling them in summer school."

"You're not alone on that one," said Ruth. "Look at all these tutoring centres springing up all over town. Sylvan Learning Centres has seen its revenues in Canada grow by more than 30 percent since 1994. And that growth is dependent on the boomers' insecurity about whether their kids are going to be prepared for the working world. My thinking is that kids need to be kids — for the summer, at least!"

"Despite my concerns, I agree. I remember my care-free summer holidays as a kid," I replied. "Hey, they'll have years to be grown-ups, right?"

"Exactly! Your children probably won't challenge your desire that they continue their educations," Ruth continued. "Certain academics argue that the children of the boomers are natural-born conformists — unlike the boomers, who were born to rebel."

"Why do the boomers have the monopoly on this rebellious reputation?" I asked.

"Good question. An MIT scientist, Frank Sulloway, chalks it up to birth order. Firstborns, he argues, tend to identify with parents and authority more than later-borns do. Because the baby-boom families were so much larger than those that preceded and followed them, there's a much higher percentage of rebellious, nonconformist later-borns in the generation of boomers. Now that we're back to smaller families, the percentage of firstborns is way up — these characters like the status quo. That study of U.S. freshmen provided another interesting statistic to support Sulloway's thesis. Back in the 1970s, the most important objective for college freshmen was to develop a meaningful philosophy of life. Do you know what it is now?" Ruth inquired.

I shook my head.

"They want to make money. Nearly three-quarters of them said their most important objective is to be very well off financially."

"In a way, I'm not surprised by that response. Our culture values material possessions more than commitment to principles and philosophies," I said. "The statistics on volunteering show that young people are active volunteers, and one of their main motivators is the job experience volunteering provides."

"Do you have time for a second coffee?" Ruth asked.

"I do, and I'd like to talk to you about my friend Sharon," I said.

We sat over our coffee, talking quietly about Sharon and her cancer. I told Ruth that I would be travelling down to Toronto within the next two weeks to accompany her to chemotherapy sessions at Sunnybrook Hospital. We talked about the changes and increased demands that the boomers — the aging boomers — will be bringing to Canada's health care system. We talked about the nature of friendship. Ruth told me that I could expect to see more of this — she'd helped several friends battle cancer. We shed our tears, thinking of our friends.

We talked a bit more about community. I told Ruth that Pieter and I had been contemplating taking the plunge and buying a house. We talked about our attachment to the Glebe, how it had become our home, the place we found many friends. When I told her about the possibility that we might buy Frank and Jean's home, Ruth launched into one of her sermons about synchronicity — her belief that things happen when and how they're supposed to happen. We just have to be ready to run with the ball. *Carpe diem* — seize the day.

"As much as I'd like to sit here and chat away the afternoon, I should be getting back to the library," I said, draining my coffee cup. "I'd like to finish up some research for Hazen. I'm seeing him tomorrow." We began clearing away our trays.

"On the way back, I want you to listen to something that proves my point about the boomers' kids. Dylan sent me this CD by the rap stars Public Enemy. He said there might be something on it I'd be interested in. In his note, he told me that the songs were the soundtrack for a new movie called *He Got Game*, about a young ghetto kid who gets an opportunity to play pro basketball and make millions of bucks. All about money, in other words."

"So why did Dylan send you the CD? I don't get it," I said. We stacked our trays and walked to Ruth's car.

"Well, you can listen for yourself. This newfangled Beetle has a CD player in it. My first Bug didn't even have a radio. Pretty fancy, eh?" she said, pushing the CD into the player. From the speakers came an unmistakable '60s tune — "There is something happening here, What it is ain't exactly clear . . . It's time to stop children, what's that sound, everybody look what's goin' down." The song had kept its guitar riffs and cool sound, but it was now wrapped in a heavy layer of rap music.

I said, "I remember that song. My older brothers had the album. It's Buffalo Springfield, I think."

"Good memory. The song is called 'For What It's Worth.' It hit the U.S. Top 10 in 1967. And it was inspired by teenage riots on Los Angeles's Sunset Strip. It's considered one of the best protest songs of the sixties. If you listen to the lyrics of the original, it's truly revolutionary. I should be able to remember this song. I was doing my graduate work at Berkeley when it hit the charts. I must have listened to it a thousand times. Dylan said he thought this new version would be a real trip down memory lane for me." She laughed. She sang softly about battle lines and everybody being wrong.

"I think it's kind of weird that I listened to the same songs my kids are listening to today," I commented as Ruth navigated back to the StatsCan library.

"Well, the song is actually less rebellious in this version than it was in your day, Meredith. Granted, it has a couple of foul words in it that weren't in the original, but listen to the lyrics," she said as the group rapped.

"Are you ready for the real revolution which is the evolution of the mind," sang Public Enemy. The song went on to talk about love conquering all. Definitely a softer message. But more disturbing in a way. Much of the new version was devoted to asking how the human race got itself into such a mess where, as Public Enemy continued, "folks don't even own themselves."

"You know," I said as Ruth pulled up in front of the library, "I think this song is about community — specifically, our *lack* of focus on the collective needs of our friends, family and neighbours."

"I thought the same thing," replied Ruth, pensively. "I think that's the reason Dylan sent it to me. He wants me to think about the fact that love conquers all."

"It's not exactly the war between the generations any longer. It's more like a heated discussion between us and our kids," I stated.

"I think that, in many ways, we're just postponing our generation gap," replied Ruth. "Kids growing up today are less concerned with flower power. They know that knowledge is power. We're going to see a generation gap as the boomers age and begin to cost society money — health care, government pensions, that sort of thing. We've got to wonder whether our kids are going to want to fund our old age. I'm not so certain they will."

"Another good reason for boomers to start saving in earnest," I said. "I'll have to add that to Hazen's list!"

9

I'd Like to Teach the World to...

The morning after Canada Day, I reported for work, still tired from the previous night's fireworks extravaganza on Parliament Hill.

Dylan opened the door this morning. "Hey, it's the lady who stole the chair and table from my bedroom!" Now that woke me up and, before I knew what was happening, I found myself engulfed in his bear hug.

"I'm happy to see you too, Dylan." I laughed and gave him a kiss on the cheek. "When did you get in?"

"We crossed the bridge at Buffalo yesterday. Appropriate, don't you think? I celebrated my homecoming on Canada Day." He laughed. "Then I discover half the furniture's gone from my room."

"What can I say?" I replied. "I promise that I'll give it back when I'm finished my contract for your dad.

Speaking of your dad, is he around? We're supposed to be working this morning."

"He's still eating his breakfast, Meredith. I guess I kept him up kind of late last night. We got talking and before we knew it, it was way after midnight." He led me into the kitchen. "I guess Mom and Dad have told you that they're pretty concerned that I've decided to come home for a while," he said in a hushed, serious tone.

I nodded.

"I hope you're telling them to relax," he said.

Once again, I nodded. We shared a complicit smile as we entered the kitchen to find Hazen sipping his coffee.

Hazen had asked me to gather a few salient facts about global demographics — facts that he could use in his seminar to illustrate the growing importance of the worldwide bazaar that experts call "the global market-place."

"What many people don't realize is that the population boom is behind us here in Canada," he told me as we were preparing to research the topic. "We, like many industrialized countries, including the United States, France, Italy and Germany, are facing a 'birth dearth.' Our demographic future is one of slow growth and growing older. If fertility remains at the current level of 1.7 births per woman, we're going to see a decline in our population. In the future, we'll be relying on immigration to make our population grow. Then there's the aging issue. We're living longer. And that means more seniors. In 1960, seniors accounted for about 8 percent of the population. Courtesy of the healthy boomers, by 2020 seniors will make up nearly 20 percent of the population."

"I don't understand why you're focusing on Canada's demographic structure when you want me to research global demographics," I said.

"It's *because* of our demographic condition that we must look beyond our borders at the rest of the world," Hazen explained. "The continued health of our economy and our companies is based on expanding markets. It's all about growth. But it becomes pretty challenging to 'grow' a company when your market is, at best, growing slowly or, at worst, shrinking. And that's what's happening not only in Canada but also in the United States, which happens to be our largest trading partner. This situation is forcing many Canadian and American companies to look beyond North America for markets with growth potential. And that's why we need to know about what's happening to populations around the world. In fact, many stock market experts have pointed out that stocks in North American companies that are globally exposed — that is, they sell their products outside of North America — have, in recent years, outperformed companies that are more domestically exposed."

"Okay, I understand. So, when I'm looking at this topic, my focus should be on what global demographics mean to our North American economy," I said.

"Right. In the past, I've told my audiences about how the North American baby boom affected our economy. It's time to expand that story," Hazen concluded.

I headed off to the Ottawa Public Library. And I found

plenty of information on what's happening to the world's population. After a morning's research, I reviewed my notes. I certainly had uncovered an interesting collection of factoids. But I still had no way of linking that information to our North American economy.

Human beings, I learned, have been around for at least one million years. It took 990,000 of those years for the world's population to grow to the size of New York City. Then, boom! In the past 40 years, the world's population had doubled, up from nearly 3 billion in 1955 to almost 6 billion today. It's estimated that barring huge disasters — war or pestilence, for example — that number will hit 8 billion by 2025. The vast majority of the continuing increase is taking place in the less-developed nations; nine out of every ten persons being added to the world's population live in Third World countries.

The key to all this growth is increasing life expectancy. People are living significantly longer lives all around the world. Longevity was once the domain of developed countries but, since World War II, medical and public health technology has been available in nearly all countries. Whereas our population grew dramatically back in the 1950s and '60s courtesy of a baby boom, the populations of less-developed countries are growing today because the risk of death has been lowered dramatically. The average Indian woman today may still have three children, a bundle by Canadian standards, but down from five in 1980. And life expectancy in India has risen from 52 to 60 in the same period.

The gap is closing between rich and poor countries. In the past 35 years, the developing world extended its average life expectancy by sixteen years, while industrialized countries added only five years. Although life is still very difficult in many less-developed countries, the UN Food and Agricultural Organization reports that malnutrition has dropped from a historical norm of 35 percent to under 20 percent in the past 40 years.

This means we will continue to see profound growth in many less-developed countries. Ottawa will see its population creep up from 1 million to 1.2 million between 1995 and 2015. That's an increase of 22 percent. Then look at Hohhot, a Chinese city with 1.1 million inhabitants in 1995. By 2015, Hohhot's population will be 1.8 million — a 70 percent jump. But for real growth, watch Lusaka, Zambia. That city will mushroom from 1.4 million in 1995 to 2.9 million in 2015 — an astounding explosion of over 100 percent.

Two-thirds of all the people in the world live on only 40 percent of the earth's land surface. Travel to China (the fastest-growing country in the world) or the Indian subcontinent and you'll begin to understand the concept of population density. More than 40 percent of the world's population lives in these areas of Asia, where you'll find nearly 400 people live on each square mile of land. China's population is some 41 times larger than Canada's. Imagine our population of 30 million evenly spread over Canada's 10 million square kilometres. We'd be a pretty lonely bunch.

Despite our status as demographic pipsqueaks, Canada sports the Western world's seventh-largest economy. Our prosperity depends on our place in the world's markets — from foreign investors buying our stocks, bonds and currency to what our companies sell abroad. In the 1990s, the growth of exports was the "tide that lifted all boats," according to Statistics Canada. From 1991 to 1994, Canada had the fastest growth of any of the G7 nations in the share of its economy devoted to exports. Not surprising for a small nation in the orbit of a very large U.S. market. Continued prosperity depends on continuing trade in the global marketplace.

By mid-afternoon, I had assembled a fascinating collection of tidbits that, taken together, presented an unmistakable message: the future growth of our economy and our companies depends on looking outside of our borders. But it wasn't until I picked up a newspaper that I had a framework to make those statistics into an interesting story that Hazen could use in his seminar.

"New Coke Company Aims to Open Eastern Throats" read the headline above the article describing how Coke is poised to lift its "share of throat" in the emerging economies of Europe's former communist bloc. Interesting, but what really caught my eye was one number — one billion. Coke sells one billion servings of its products around the world *every single day!* The math was simple but the answer amazing. Today — and every day — one in six people on this planet will consume a Coca-Cola Co. product.

I was reminded of a story my friend Janis told me when she returned from a recent trip to Costa Rica. She recounted a day spent travelling by water taxi up a remote river through uninhabited jungles. No people, just untouched scenery and startlingly beautiful birds. The boat rounded a bend in the river to reveal a Coke sign perched on stilts in the river. "I didn't know whether to be amazed or disgusted at the near-complete penetration of Coke into every corner of the globe," she told me.

All this started me thinking about having a cold Coke. It was about three and I needed a break. But before I headed for the door, I snooped around the stacks and found a couple of books about Coca-Cola and its history. I checked them out and headed for the chip wagon on the corner and bought my Coke. Then I settled onto a park bench and opened my drink and my books.

"'I've been experimenting on a little preparation,'" I read. "'A kind of decoction nine-tenths water and the other tenth drugs that don't cost more than a dollar a barrel . . . The third year we could easily sell 1,000,000 bottles in the United States — a profit of at least $350,000 — and then it would be time to turn our attention toward the real idea of the business . . . Why, our headquarters would be in Constantinople and our hindquarters in Further India! . . . Annual income — well, God only knows how many millions and millions!'" In 1873, Mark Twain wrote those words — pure fiction — about the creation of a beverage. Not only was he a wit and a storyteller but he was also profoundly prescient.

It wasn't until 1886 that Dr. John Styth Pemberton introduced Coca-Cola to the world as a headache remedy and nerve tonic. By the 1930s, the drink had permeated the American consciousness to represent everything good about God, country and capitalism in the United States of America. Today, Coke is the world's most widely distributed product and "Coca-Cola" is the most universally recognized word on earth, with the exception of "OK."

But Twain had a couple of details wrong. Coca-Cola Co.'s sales are in the stratosphere, exceeding $18.5 billion, with an operating profit close to $4 billion — far more than the millions and millions he imagined. And those sales reflect a solid understanding of the demographics of the entire planet.

This information led me back into the library, where I scouted out everything I could find about Coca-Cola — annual reports, articles in *Fortune*, *Time*, *Newsweek*. As I searched, Hazen's words echoed in my brain. It may be different this time, but certain things never change. And the need to learn about the fundamentals of a company is a constant.

Spurred by waves of immigration, the American population grew from 50 million in 1880 to more than 90 million by 1910. Although they didn't have much money, the immigrants had a taste for things American, and that included the nickel Coke. Savvy marketing, including ornate soda fountains and the trademark curvy bottle, made the new drink a success. By 1905, Coca-Cola had kicked its cocaine habit and in 1919, the company went public. (Sun Trust Bank acquired Coke shares back in 1919 for $110,000. Those shares are now worth well over $1 billion.)

The Depression years were rough on many American businesses, but Coke thrived, selling a product that picked up people's spirits for very little cash. During the depths of this difficult decade its stock price rose, from $20 in 1932 to $160 in 1937. And Coke began looking around the world to countries like Cuba, Canada and Germany for new customers. Coke executives put the push on to expand into overseas markets, starting a program of building bottling plants worldwide.

But it was World War II that cemented Coke's worldwide reputation. Coke executives were standing at the ready to take advantage of the near-religious significance that Coke assumed for American soldiers fighting overseas. Legendary company president Robert Woodruff ordered: "We will see that every man in uniform gets a bottle of Coca-Cola for five cents, wherever he is and whatever it costs our company." Smart move. Coca-Cola emerged from the war with a worldwide network of 64 bottling plants. In 1950, *Time* magazine reported that one-third of the company's profits came from abroad. By 1972, foreign earnings had eclipsed Coke's domestic income.

In the 1980s, Roberto Goizueta, then the chairman of Coca-Cola, pointed out that Americans accounted for less than 5 percent of the world's population. Why, he asked rhetorically, wouldn't Coke be focusing on 95 percent of the market, particularly when Coke still had to gain so much "share of throat" in foreign lands? Today, Coke sees approximately 80 percent of its profit from overseas markets.

Coca-Cola Co. has marketed its product brilliantly. It sells the American experience that the rest of the world is desperate to attain. Yet the company takes pains to integrate itself into its target culture. In Japan, a country known for its work ethic, "the pause that refreshes" became "the moment that refreshes." And Coke is always there sniffing out an opportunity. In 1989, when the Berlin Wall fell, Coke employees were present, handing out free Cokes. Until the fall of communism, Pepsi was the undisputed leader in eastern and central Europe. Communism is now gone and "Coke is it," outselling Pepsi two-to-one in the region. It continues to build that market, placing cooler cabinets and vending machines throughout those countries in a bid to raise consumption to levels seen in western Europe. They see the demographic potential of countries such as Ukraine, a nation of 50 million people, where only 18 servings per person were consumed last year. In nearby Austria, 150 servings per head were downed. Lots of Cokes yet to be sold by the company that sees water as its main competitor.

But the demographic bonanza — the biggest market of them all — is China. And Coke is in.

China, with more than 1.2 billion people, is poised to make the great leap forward into economic reforms, privatizing state-owned enterprises. Housing reforms, for example, will transform millions of Chinese into homeowners for the first time in their lives. Until recently, almost all urban housing was built and owned by the state. This change has the potential to radically alter the Chinese economy much as home ownership transformed American society from the 1930s to the 1960s, creating a house-proud middle class with lots of disposable income to spend on consumer goods. All of this is music to Coke's ears.

Doug Ivester is Coke's current CEO and chairman. His aim is to double worldwide consumption of Coke. And China is critical to that goal. China is now Coke's eighth-largest market. The company's strategy to get a bottle of Coke into the hands of every Chinese person depends on the Communist Party. In Shanghai, neighbourhood committees made up of senior citizens have been signed up by Coke to sell to the families they supervise on behalf of the Communist Party.

Ivester has transformed his company into a technological machine capable of monitoring its far-flung empire with speed and ease. It previously took more than two months to retrieve information from around the world. Now it takes a couple of days. The new Coke Card, used for discounts and freebies at places like movie theatres, allows the company to collect instant information on the who, what, when and where of a purchase of a bottle of Coke.

There are only a couple of challenges to Coke's bottom line. One is the currently strong U.S. dollar. Weak foreign currencies suppress the growth of the company. Another challenge is faltering global economies. But is Ivester worried? No way. He sees these issues as short-term problems. All you have to do is look at the big picture — and China, with 1 billion potential Coke consumers, is a very big picture. I knew Hazen, with his focus on long-term investing, would approve of Ivester's response when asked about foreign currency concerns: "We are not managing for the next quarter."

So I told him my Coke story, sparing no details. I knew I had hit paydirt when I finished up with Ivester's quote about Coke's long-term objectives.

"Not only does the Coke story introduce people to what's going on with the world's population but it does it in a way that everyone can relate to. We all drink Coke, after all." He laughed. "This approach allows me to introduce into my seminar other North American companies that are paying attention to global demographics."

"What do you have in mind?" I asked.

"During your research, did you by any chance come across any of Peter Drucker's comments on global demographics?" asked Hazen.

"He's an economist, a management guru, right? No, I didn't. What does he have to say about the subject?"

"I like the way Drucker thinks. He says that demographics are the single most important factor that nobody pays attention to. I agree, and I hope with my new seminar we can get more people to hear the message," said Hazen. "Actually, Drucker makes many of the same points you just did — that the number and proportion of younger people is rapidly shrinking in developed countries like ours, for example. Drucker worries that this growing older population will put a heavy burden on younger workers to support their elders. But Drucker also examines the relative strength of North American companies to European and Japanese companies. He argues that companies in North America and Britain are run for the benefit of shareholders — shareholders who constantly pressure for higher returns, whereas companies in other countries — Germany, France, Italy and Japan — are managed not for return to shareholders but for return to insiders of the company. Those insiders could be the management of these foreign companies, powerful families or government bodies."

"It's not difficult to see why North American stocks are a more valuable investment for shareholders," I commented.

"No kidding. And that's one of the reasons the North American stock markets have done so well over the past few years. If North American companies don't deliver, maximizing stockholder value, management is out on its ear. And that desire to deliver to shareholders has led North American companies into the global marketplace. As the North American population ages, future growth is offshore. Look at Coke. The U.S. will export its own ideas to other large powers. For now, the North American economy leads the pack."

"I think I see where you're going here," I said. "You're going to combine these two threads. One, North American companies are more desirable to investors because they're managed for shareholders. Two, to continue providing the solid returns that those investors demand, North American companies must grow their companies, and one way of doing that is by going global. For many companies faced with shrinking domestic markets, expanding overseas is the only way. Now we're looking at a virtuous circle — people all over the world want to own shares in North American companies, demographics dictates that many of these companies must sell into growing foreign markets, this global expansion makes North American companies even more attractive to investors."

"Very good," said Hazen with a smile. "I couldn't have said it better. And I think that Canadian investors would be interested in learning about how Bombardier, the Montreal-based manufacturer of transportation and aerospace products, has built on its knowledge of what's happening around the world to transform itself into an $8.5-billion-a-year company. Let me see," he said, searching through his file drawers. "I have a file right here on Bombardier."

"I think of snowmobiles when you mention Bombardier," I said.

"That was the starting point of this company. J.A. Bombardier built his first snowmobile in the garage of his father's farm in 1922, when he was only 15 years old. The company has travelled many miles since then. In 1974, it diversified into the transit equipment industry, building rolling stock for the Montreal subway. In 1986, it moved into the aerospace industry when it acquired Canadair, an aircraft manufacturer. The company recently has taken off into foreign markets, now deriving nearly 90 percent of its revenues from outside Canada. Recognizing the growth potential of foreign markets, it created a subsidiary, Bombardier International, with the sole mandate of researching and identifying new markets."

"Very much like Coke's history. They recognized that to achieve the growth they wanted they'd have to leave their country of birth," I added. "You know, Bombardier and Coke are complementary stories. Coke sells a product that consumers *want*. At a dollar a drink, it's an impulse purchase. But Bombardier sells what countries and companies *need*. Two different marketing strategies oriented to the global market."

"Good point. And, because Bombardier kept an eye on what the people of the world needed, they met with huge success. Here's an example," he said, pulling a paper from the file. "Here's an article on Bombardier aerospace. The company has focused on manufacturing regional aircraft, mid-size planes that carry commuters on short runs that are not economically feasible using large jets. A very smart market to be in these days."

"I get it," I said. "With the boom in business travel, they're selling to all the smaller airlines that handle the short commuter hops."

"Exactly. Travel now accounts for the second highest business expense following payroll on corporate ledgers. Regional airlines are having great years, with growth rates twice as high as the big airlines'. And Bombardier's order book is crammed full — orders increased by more than 50 percent in 1997, with sales to all corners of the world, everywhere from Slovenia to Papua New Guinea. Now, like Coke, they're poised to take on the Chinese market. They recognize that China is one of the world's largest markets for rail transportation equipment. So it comes as no surprise that Bombardier is working on a joint venture to manufacture rail transit vehicles for the China ministry of railways."

"What you're saying makes such good sense, but I can hear the naysayers in the crowd saying: 'What if?' What if the Japanese economy sinks into a depression? What if China devalues its currency? What if political instability destroys Indonesia's economy? What if Russia is consumed by inflation?"

"And those people are quite right," said Hazen. "There is going to be turmoil in the global marketplace. Things are different these days. Countries like Russia are experimenting with a capitalist-style economy, for example. There are bound to be many blunders until they get it right. But if you visit Russia these days, you'll see the benefits of a North American–style economy — stores are now filled with goods. Young and middle-aged Russians don't want to go back to the bad old days of communism. If we can look beyond today's noise, we can see much better times ahead for countries like Russia. The collapse of communism around the world holds enormous potential for our businesses — huge new markets have opened before our eyes. We must not overlook the current numbers. The growth in world trade has consistently exceeded the growth in the world's GDP. What's behind wealth creation in the world today? The answer is simple: world trade."

"That's the big picture, Hazen," I stated. "How do you know whether the company you're investing in won't get caught in a global meltdown?"

"I prefer to be a cautious optimist," he answered. "I like to see a company act that way too. And I see companies like Coke and Bombardier spreading their risk. They realize that the countries with the biggest upside potential also have the biggest downside risk. As a result, companies like these are not putting all their eggs in one country's basket. They're expanding into many foreign jurisdictions. That's what I like to see."

Ruth stuck her head into the room. "What do you like to see?"

"I'd like to see you, Ruth," said Hazen. "Come on in. Meredith and I are just finishing up."

Ruth said, "I dropped by to talk to Dylan but he seems to be out. I wondered if you and Dylan wanted to join me for dinner."

"Sure, that sounds great. I'd made no dinner plans," replied Hazen.

"Why don't you come over around seven-thirty. So, I bet you were talking about aging populations around the world," commented Ruth, turning to look at me.

"Yes, that was one of our topics," I replied.

"People don't understand how old the world is becoming," she said.

"And hopefully wiser?" I asked.

Ruth laughed. "I don't know about that. Japan and some of the European countries are becoming positively ancient. Look at Italy, for example. There are about 60 million Italians today. If they keep reproducing at the current rate, by the end of the next century they'll be down to 20 million."

"We're actually a much younger country than many," said Hazen. "But age is going to catch up with us eventually, too."

"You can really see how the world is aging if you look at the history of immigration to this country," commented Ruth. "Back in the 1950s, '60s and '70s, we saw waves of immigrants from Britain and northern and southern Europe. Back then, those were young countries, full of 20-year-olds who wanted better lives for themselves. And Canada offered that hope. Now we're seeing increasing numbers of immigrants coming from Asian countries, including India, Taiwan, China and Pakistan. You wait — the next big wave of immigrants will be heading here from Africa."

"Canada really is a global village," I said. "I was surprised by the number of immigrants — more than half of Canada's population growth in the first five years of the 1990s was attributable to international migration."

"We're seeing about 225,000 immigrants arrive in Canada yearly," said Hazen. "Surprisingly, before World War I, we had upwards of 400,000 immigrants arriving on our shores each year. We've actually reduced our immigration rate since the 1950s. There will come a time, as Canada's population ages, that immigration may again be the vital force it once was. We're going to have plenty of 20-year-olds entering the workplace in the first decade of the 2000s as the echo boomers finish school and start landing jobs. But, as Bill Sterling and Stephen Waite point out in *Boomernomics*, we start having problems when hordes of boomers begin retiring in the 2020s. They're predicting intergenerational warfare as the echo kids balk at supporting the aging boomers. Who's going to work to pay for the boomers' pension entitlements, their health care needs? That may be the time when immigration becomes a key government policy."

"The government seems to be laying the groundwork for this," Ruth pointed out. "According to government reports, they're unequivocal about Canada's interest in admitting immigrants who will waste no time in becoming involved in economic activities. In other words, immigrants will arrive and produce, stand and deliver!"

"More differences for your 'this time it's different' theme," I said to Hazen.

"But our discussion is really about aging and the constant, undeniable fact that each year we become a year older," he replied. "'Youth is a religion from which one always ends up being converted,' to quote André Malraux. Ah well, nothing that a good cup of tea can't solve," Hazen said and invited us to join him in the kitchen.

10

Homefronts

"I'd like to ask you a favour of a rather personal sort," said Hazen.

I'd picked up the phone wondering who would be calling me at seven-thirty on a Tuesday morning. School was out, the kids were still in bed. I knew it wouldn't be their friends.

"A favour?" I asked. "At this hour in the morning?" We both laughed.

"I knew you'd be up," he said. "It's something I'd like you to bring to work with you this morning."

"So, what's this personal thing you'd like?"

"Your grocery list," he answered. "I know you keep one. I've seen the pad of paper on the counter beside your fridge."

"Are you planning on buying groceries for a crowd of teenagers? Because that's the kind of stuff I have on my list. Malcolm's pals are always here, eating me out of house and home. Sure, I'll bring it along. But you have to promise to tell me why you want it."

"No problem," replied Hazen. "Dissecting your grocery list is going to be your project for the week."

"I thought work was going to take me away from my domestic chores!" I said. "Hazen, while we're on the subject of favours, I've got to ask you for some time off. Sharon's husband phoned last night. She's scheduled for a course of chemotherapy next week. He asked me if I could stay with her in Toronto and take her to the hospital for her treatments. He's going to stay in Guelph with their kids — they're trying to keep things on the home front as normal as possible. I know this is right in the middle of everything." My voice tapered off. Why did everything always seem to happen at once? I had my recurring feeling of being pulled in 17 directions simultaneously.

"Meredith, it's absolutely no problem. We'll catch up when you're back. In fact, I think Dylan, Ruth and I are heading down to Stratford for a couple of plays next weekend. That means I'll be missing a couple of days at the end of the week. You know my theme: keep your eye on the long run. This is a short-term interruption. But, for Sharon's sake, it's one you must attend to," said Hazen firmly.

A few hours later I arrived at his door, grocery list in hand.

"So," I said, holding up my list. "What's this all about?"

Once we were settled in his office, he began. "Last week we tackled global demographics and the ways companies can thrive in the global environment. This week, I want us to look at the characteristics of companies that excel in the domestic environment. In other words, what makes companies that operate in Canada successful? What qualities should an investor be looking for? We know that boomers have played a key role in the health of many domestic businesses."

"Right, it's the Gerber baby food example that you speak about in your current seminar. Millions of extra babies — the boomers — came along in the 1950s and '60s. All consumed baby food and, together, they significantly improved the health of that company," I said.

"That's it. But the real trick," Hazen explained, "is figuring out where the boomers are going, what they're going to hit next. Some sectors are easy to foresee. As boomers start preparing for retirement, they're going to need more financial services. Health care is another hot ticket. Aging boomers equal increasing demands on the health care system. Boomers are going to have more free time on their hands as their kids grow up and leave home — that bodes favourably for the travel and entertainment industries."

"How on earth does my grocery list factor into this?" I asked.

"The food industry provides a superb example of the power the boom wields over domestic industries. Boomers have fundamentally and irrevocably changed the food industry in this country. Some companies have benefited enormously from the changes the boomers have wrought. Loblaws is a good example. Its earnings per share tripled within the past five years. An integral part of their business savvy has been their ability to keep their eyes on the boomers in a way competitors have missed," said Hazen.

"I do a fair bit of my shopping at Loblaws," I said. "At the one over by Pretoria Bridge. They have great President's Choice products. In fact, look at my list. I have a couple of President's Choice items listed by name. Pieter loves their Salmon Wellington and the kids ask for Pad Thai all the time. I think they'd eat it every night, given the chance."

"I want you to look at the characteristics that Loblaws has developed and select those that make for a successful retailer in this country. That skill set is what an investor should be looking for when they're going to put their money into a domestically exposed company," stated Hazen.

"That makes good sense, using Loblaws as an example. Plus, everybody understands food. Hey, we all eat!" We both laughed.

Hazen handed me a file folder that included a Loblaws 1997 Annual Report and a couple of research reports on retail industries, and then set me loose.

"Remember, I want a compelling story," he said as I headed out the door and off to the library.

Even though I knew it to be true, the pure power of the boom always amazed me. Boomers drive the retail industry in North America. Period. The value of the retail trade in Canada is huge — $211.2 billion in 1995, according to Statistics Canada. And the big buyers are the boomers.

Boomers, who make up well over 40 percent of

Canada's population, are at or near their peak earning years, and many still have young children at home or are still supporting older ones. They are the nation's grocery buyers. It's a pretty simple equation: determine what boomers want or need and you've made a sale. That's exactly what Loblaws did, and continues to do. This is a company whose strategy is planted in the future as opposed to rooted in the past.

"Here's the story I've got for you," I said to Hazen when I returned to his office on Friday. "You're going to love it. The boomers are the main characters."

"Go ahead," Hazen said. "Sounds as if I *will* like it."

"Loblaws, like the other grocers in this country, had to innovate," I began. "They had their backs against the wall. They knew that Wal-Mart was coming to town. All they had to do was look south of the border to see the power of America's discount dynamo. Wal-Mart is the number-two grocer in the States and they weren't even in the grocery market a decade ago. That's one tough competitor. Unlike many other Canadian grocers, Loblaws was quick off the mark."

"All retailers in this country have to be on their toes these days," said Hazen. "Wal-Mart is not the only big-box game in town. Look at what's happening in the home renovation trade — all these big stores like Home Depot and Rona. That's tough for the little guys and even some of the big guys. Beaver Lumber closed its stores in Ottawa. It can't compete with the big-box boys, so it's going to focus its operations on smaller communities."

"Loblaws looked at the demographics and positioned their stores and products accordingly," I said.

"Give me some examples," said Hazen.

"Let's look at what the trade calls their 'controlled labels.' These are their private brands — President's Choice, no frills, Too Good To Be True. All are geared to households where there's very little time to cook. They're convenience foods aimed at households where both parents work. Sound familiar?"

"That's the boomers, all right," replied Hazen with a chuckle.

"But there's more. The studies show that boomers are more likely than those in the preceding generation to buy prepared foods. But boomers want more. They're very demanding, in fact. They want something better than those TV dinners of old. Remember those unappetizing, dried-out turkey dinners in aluminum trays? Forget it. Boomers want good-tasting jambalaya, Vietnamese spring rolls and Mexican chimichangas. But there's more. Boomers pride themselves on being savvy shoppers, on getting the most for the money. So not only does the product have to taste good and be sophisticated, it has to be the best quality for the price. And here's where Loblaws scored. By offering their own products rather than selling those of another company, they can increase their profit margins. In fact, experts estimate that private label sales in the packaged goods categories accounted for as much as 35 percent of Loblaws' sales."

"So, they offered boomers good quality and reasonable prices. That's a winning combination," mused Hazen.

"But there's much, much more," I continued. "Offering

those private labels meant they actually reduced the number of products the stores needed to stock. Instead of offering 12 different varieties of mustards, you'll notice that Loblaws offers only a few selections. They just happen to be the right ones. Now studies show that boomers want the stress of shopping reduced. Offering fewer choices is a smart — and cost-effective — way to reduce stress. Boomers also want shopping made physically easier. Loblaws has done that too. If you're looking for dessert products, for example, you'll find them all together in a Loblaws store. Frozen desserts are together with fresh ones. Unlike other stores, where there is only one frozen food section, at Loblaws there are freezers all over the store. Makes it easier for those busy boomers who are rushing in at the end of their work day searching for something to satisfy their sweet tooth," I concluded.

"Does your grocery list support what you've been telling me?" asked Hazen.

"It sure does. Like I told you earlier this week, I had a couple of President's Choice products on my list. I also had a bag of salad on my list. I wouldn't have had that on my list 10 years ago because it wasn't invented. In the old days, I bought a head of lettuce. Now, I buy it prepackaged, prewashed, ready for me to simply toss in the salad bowl. Prepackaged salads are now a $2-billion business in North America. And Loblaws is poised to get into this corner of the business too. They're expanding from selling frozen dinners to selling fresh and ready-to-serve meals — 'home-meal replacements,' they're called. Loblaws refers to them as 'home meal solutions.' And boomers want their problems solved. Look at the American numbers: 22 percent of U.S. consumers bought ready-made food from supermarkets in 1997. That was nearly double the number buying these meals just a year before. You can bet those numbers will come to Canada if the product is offered. Loblaws promises that their products will be distinguished from others available in the Canadian market. In fact, they've established a relationship with the high-end Mövenpick restaurant chain in order to nail this market!" I chuckled.

"In general terms, then, this means aiming products directly at the boomer market and, most important, paying attention to what boomers need," said Hazen.

"Exactly," I replied. "But it's not only what boomers need, it's also what they *want*," I added. "Loblaws has paid attention to that too. You and I both know that boomers are more likely than previous generations to take materialism and convenience as rights. As a result, they're always on the lookout for things that can make their lives better, more comfortable. Loblaws has wisely played on these psychic desires," I said, pulling out a copy of *President's Choice Magazine*. "Although the masthead carefully states that the views in the magazine do not necessarily reflect the opinions of Loblaws, this magazine is a very elaborate and sophisticated advertising tool for the company. And it tells boomers how to live a more graceful, interesting life — using Loblaws products, of course."

"Do you pay for it?" Hazen asked.

"Absolutely," I said. "It sells for $1.95. But it's got such great recipes and articles that I don't mind paying to receive Loblaws' advertising. Wild, eh?"

"Mind if I take a look?" said Hazen.

I handed it to him and he flipped through it.

"Look at this," he said, holding the magazine aloft. "An ad for the new banking services they're offering."

"Yes, I was just going to get to that. This is part of making life easier. You can do your banking at the same time as you grocery shop. Plus, you earn grocery points, which translate into a discount on your purchases," I explained. "The investment analysts love it, suggesting that the earnings contribution of the banking service could be substantial. But that's not all the investment analysts like about Loblaws."

"Go on," said Hazen.

"Remember I said earlier that Loblaws not only positioned their products in accordance with the boomers' needs and wants but they also positioned their stores that way? They've paid careful attention to neighbourhood demographics when choosing locations for their stores. Loblaws operates under several different banners, including no frills, Real Canadian Superstore and SuperCentre. Each caters to a different economic stratum in society. The superstores, which go head-to-head with the big-box outlets like Costco, appeal to the bargain hunters among us. The Loblaws I frequent is geared to the upper end of the income scale. The management has also very cleverly put the money they've made back into the ground. Unlike other grocers, Loblaws owns a lot of the real estate under their stores. By ploughing money back into the business, they've made their segment of the business sustainable. They can weather the competition that Wal-Mart is bringing onto the Canadian scene."

"Loblaws' approach reminds me very much of the Gap's," remarked Hazen. "Be everywhere. Be everything to all people, particularly the boomers. Make shopping easy. Elevate the ordinary."

"Everywhere, everything, easy, elevate," I mused. "Loblaws is certainly everywhere. They've saturated the market and now they're moving full steam ahead into Quebec and western Canada. So they still have plenty of room for growth. They are everything to their shoppers. Not only can you buy your groceries there, you can also do your banking, pick up your photographs, get a prescription filled. One-stop shopping! And they've made it oh-so-easy. Loblaws has elevated a frozen dinner into a gourmet experience, something you could actually serve at a dinner party. That's what the boomers are looking for in every retail market they touch — everywhere, everything, easily and elevated."

"You're going to see plenty of retailers following Loblaws' path," said Hazen. Look at what's happening with Eaton's, the Bay and Sears. They've all pumped millions into facelifts and reshifted their focus. I'd put my money on Sears, actually. They're well into the everything, everywhere, easily and elevated mantra that boomers love. Like Loblaws, it has a well-known line of private labels, including Kenmore and Craftsman. Between their catalogue service and dealer network, they can reach virtually anybody in Canada. They sell everything from diapers to dryers to diamonds. And they're in the midst of making themselves look better, more fashionable."

"And Sears is keeping an eye on the boomers' need for

ease. I've read they're expanding their home service division," I remarked.

"That's a smart move on their part. The overall service market is well over $10 billion. Sears currently has about $270 million of it. There's a lot of room for growth there, and Sears has the name and reputation to move into the market in a big way."

"So, does our 4-E formula of everything, everywhere, easily and elevated work for all businesses that sell to the boomers?" I asked.

"Let's give it a shot," replied Hazen. "Name a successful business that's domestically based in Canada."

"How about Intrawest?" I said. "Ruth and I were talking about it the other day."

"Obviously, Intrawest can't be physically everywhere. Ski resorts do need to be near mountains. But taking that into consideration, they have a well-developed network of resorts across North America, from Whistler in B.C. to Mont Ste. Marie just north of Ottawa to resorts in Vermont, California, Colorado, New Jersey and West Virginia. Plus, they've got plans to develop a four-seasons resort in Utah — another combination of residential and commercial space. That's about got the mountains covered."

"They're definitely trying to be everything to everybody," I said. "If you go to Mont Tremblant in the autumn, for example, you see tour buses filled with seniors looking at the fall colours, boomer families hiking with their kids, older boomers on the golf course and twentysomethings bombing down the hill on mountain bikes. That's just about everybody. And it's easy too. Phone one number and you've got a hotel reservation, lift tickets, golf passes — the works."

"Then there's the elevated aspect of Intrawest," added Hazen, smiling. "Just a little pun there. Intrawest has made that little village at the base of Mont Tremblant into a tourist destination. It's packed on a summer Sunday with people listening to outdoor concerts and watching dance festivals — all the while eating ice cream, drinking beer, purchasing souvenirs. It's all about selling stuff, and Intrawest has made buying into a leisure activity. Do you know that their retail and rental revenues have soared upwards of $70 million?"

I chuckled. "That's a lot of ice cream. You know, Chapters is another good example of the 4-E formula."

"Yes, they've done for books what Intrawest did for skiing. It's a handy formula for identifying consumer-oriented companies with a healthy future. I want to incorporate it into the work we'll be doing on identifying fads versus trends in the market. We'll start on that topic when you get back from Toronto," said Hazen.

"Sounds good," I replied. "There's something else I want to talk to you about, Hazen, something I think we should include in your seminar. There's been a lot of talk about a crash or, at the very least, a correction hitting this market. The headlines in recent weeks have become more and more frenzied. And, you know me, I'm not the calmest investor in the world."

"There's no doubt, Meredith, that something's brewing," said Hazen. "But you know my strategy: buy great stuff that you can hold forever. But even great stuff has its ups and downs. The trick is holding on. And I think its going to be a tricky market for the next few months. On the world scene, we're seeing some very troubled economies — Japan, Russia, Brazil, to name three. A slowdown in the global marketplace will definitely have an impact in North America, despite our relatively healthy economies. But I take your point: you want to get working on the topic of crashes and corrections."

"I think you called that our 'Lions, Tigers and Bears' segment of the presentation."

"Yes, designed for people like you, people who aren't too sure about what the future holds," Hazen replied.

"It's an uncertain time," I said. "Look at my own world. I'm travelling to visit a sick friend. I'm parenting a cranky teenager. Pieter and I are both self-employed, with all the vagaries that go along with that status. I'm not at all sure about my future. And that doesn't feel too good."

"Well, it's time to reinforce all the good habits you've developed over the past couple of years. You've been living within your means, you've kept your debts within a reasonable range, you're planning for the future by saving and investing. You know that most people will not earn enough to retire comfortably. Retiring without enough savings is a real risk for many. The solution to this dilemma is found in what we do with the money we earn. That's where investing comes in. Yes, there are risks to investing in the market. Markets are always going to go up and down. I've been around long enough to see a few corrections along the way. Those ups and downs are what make equities yield more as an investment — the premium the market pays to the investor who can stick through some turbulent times. Meredith, life is still going to deal you a hand you never expected. The trick lies in staying calm, saving early and regularly, identifying the real risks you face, assessing your own ability to endure risk and investing accordingly."

11

Middle Age – Yikes!

I didn't need the alarm clock to wake me on Monday morning. When it shrieked at 6:30, I was already staring at the ceiling — the same thing I'd been doing virtually all night. Visions of the previous week paraded through my head, insistent and disturbing, making restful sleep impossible. I replayed the hours I spent with Sharon in the hospital hundreds of times — watching the nurse insert the intravenous tubes into her arm, staring at the cancer medication dripping, listening to Sharon talk about her fears, her hopes, her pain. Should I have done more? What should I do now that I'm home again?

I felt guilty when I returned home to my healthy family. My problems — skirmishes with Malcolm, an uncertain job situation, discontent with our rented home — suddenly seemed small, paltry, inconsequential compared to the challenges faced by Sharon's family. When I returned home on Friday, I discovered that Pieter and the kids had a wonderful time when I was in Toronto, barbecuing hot dogs, eating plenty of potato chips, drinking lots of Coke, staying up late watching junky movies.

Ruth and Hazen turned up at our door in the late afternoon on Sunday. They'd just returned from their trip to Stratford, full of news about the plays, where they'd eaten, the charming bed and breakfast they'd discovered with Dylan. Hazen informed me that he had business in Montreal on Monday, handing me a list of topics to be researched at the StatsCan library while he was out of town. Ruth had tagged along to invite me to lunch on Monday, knowing I'd be working at the library all day.

After dinner, I went to a movie with Pieter. And that movie laid the groundwork for my sleepless night, its imagery roaming through my brain for hours on end, replaying incessantly.

"Every time I have lunch with you, I seem to be tired," I said. Ruth had picked me up and we'd headed to the Upstairs Bistro, just around the corner from the library.

"Is it those darn crows again?" Ruth asked, looking up from her menu.

"No, I had something a bit more serious on my mind last night — didn't sleep a wink," I replied. "Pieter and I went to see *Saving Private Ryan*. It was an astonishing movie — violent, gruesome, touching, gentle and, ultimately, extremely moving."

"Hollywood has got you boomers figured out. You're at

that time of life where you want and need the big 'message' movie," said Ruth.

"What do you mean? It was a story about D-Day and the Second World War. Not a boomer to be seen. We were mere figments of our parents' imagination back in the mid-1940s."

"The story was about the brutality of World War II. The message is aimed at boomers and the message is a simple one: It's time to grow up and earn your spot in this world."

"How do you figure that?" I asked.

"By their sheer numbers boomers have a virtual monopoly on popular culture in North America. And they're determined to preserve that stranglehold. Have you heard of the Other Ones?" asked Ruth. I shook my head. "After Jerry Garcia died, the remaining Grateful Dead members returned to the road as the Other Ones. I read an interview with one of its members, Mickey Hart. 'We're still young,' he insisted. The guy is at least 50! And then he said: 'You can play music until the day you die. There's no music cops that come and tap you on the shoulder and say, 'Your time is up. You're too old to play music.'"

I smiled, acknowledging Ruth's long-time devotion to the late, great Jerry Garcia. "The oldsters refuse to move on and make way for the next generation. And what, by the way, do your Deadheads have to do with *Saving Private Ryan*?"

"Both appeal to boomers. Ultimately, *Saving Private Ryan* is a morality play about growing up — taking responsibility for yourself and those around you, looking past your individual self to the team, the family and beyond to the community and the country. It's about carving your place in this world. And earning the place you've carved out for yourself," explained Ruth.

"I'd agree with that, but why do you feel that's aimed at the boomers?" I asked.

"Okay — you're part of the baby-boom generation, but what's the *other* moniker for the boomers?" Ruth parried.

"Easy, the Me generation."

"There you have it." Ruth chuckled. "It's time to move beyond that. If we want to have true meaning in our lives we have to look beyond ourselves. Boomers are at an age where that recognition is sinking in. A movie like *Saving Private Ryan* feeds on that recognition. If we believe in something enough to want to make it continue beyond our death — and let's face it, the boomers are finally beginning to recognize that they're not immortal — focusing solely on our own selves is *not* the way to do it. We could believe in nearly anything: it could be family, religion, the state, whatever. If we home in only on our immediate needs, then that thing we love doesn't have a chance of surviving us. Like Tom Hanks says, 'Earn your place.' We earn our place within our families, our communities, by trying to give more than we take. It doesn't always work. Sometimes we're forced to call in our chips. But if you live your life always taking from others with no regard for their needs — well, it's not much of a life, is it?"

"I hadn't thought of the movie in that way. But everything you say is true," I said slowly.

"Have you listened to the CD James Taylor released last year?"

"We don't have it but I've heard a couple of the tracks. One's about Richard Nixon's impeachment, I think."

"That's the one," said Ruth. "The CD's called *Hourglass*. Get it? The minutes are running out. Taylor is over 50 now so he's one of the older boomers. He's singing to all those boomers following behind him. Boomers are still listening to their old rock 'n' roll favourites, including the Grateful Dead, I might add. Nearly 60 percent of boomers still like to listen to rock, after all these years. But they like to listen to 'new' rock too — something that reflects where they are in their lives today. That's what Taylor delivers. And that, I believe, is what accounts for his continued popularity. The boomers are now middle-aged and they've seen their share of troubles — job problems, divorce, kid trouble. Taylor's songs fill the bill. His music focuses on the highly personal story: love and loss, birth and death, friends, family. The thing that interests me is how rock music has changed over the past decade. It used to have a younger, harder edge. It's growing up with the boomers and shifting gears, becoming more pensive and mature along the way. James Taylor's trip through life is shared by many boomers — starting with the hippie and drug thing, moving into the failed marriage experience, parenting challenges, and recently his brother and a couple of close friends have died."

"Sounds kind of depressing. Who'd want to listen to all that?" I asked.

"That's Taylor's genius — he's got an optimistic spin on life's tough lessons. Despite all he's been through, he sees a promising future for your generation. Boomers want to hear good news — and they're also at the stage where they want to know that life has some meaning. Why do you think we're hearing so much about spirituality these days? Taylor's got a very good grip on the state of your collective mind," replied Ruth. "There was an article in the *New York Times* recently quoting Taylor talking about the boom. 'Our generation took up so much space we didn't have to refer to anything in the past.' That's what he said."

"That's a claim for the power of the boom if I ever heard one," I said.

"Exactly. The boomers are on centre stage and they're going to stay there for a number of years yet. Taylor goes on to say that he's optimistic about the future of the quality of our culture — when you folks are in your fifties and sixties and still healthy and kicking."

"It just reinforces what we see at every point in our culture. The strength of the boom seems to turn up everywhere — from movies to music to selling coffee to cars."

"Interesting you should mention coffee and cars — both boomer favourites," said Ruth. "Second Cup — it's a Canadian company, by the way — saw its profits triple this year. They know you boomers aren't as tied to the house as you were when your kids were babies."

"And Second Cup is very savvy about where it places its cafés. Look at the one they've got right in the middle of the Glebe — a perfect spot to meet a neighbour and watch the world go by," I said.

"And then there's the auto industry and the beloved boomermobile, the van. But the boomers, they are a-changin', and the car companies realize that they fall out of step with this generation at their peril. As the oldest of the boomers head into their fifties, car companies are altering their offerings. Toyota has just launched a two-door coupe — price tag around $30,000 — that they hope will encourage boomers to trade in that sport-utility vehicle that rides like a truck. And the American car companies know they have to pay attention to the fact that boomers are aging and want to return to a comfortable car. American companies dominate the truck and sport-ute market, but it's the foreign companies, like Toyota, who sell the comfortable, well-designed cars. And Chrysler's the company with the most on the line. The company that hit pay dirt with the van back in the 1980s now sells two trucks for every car. They better prepare themselves for the next stage in the boomers' driving lives or else they're going to be back begging for a bailout from Congress."

"How on earth do you know all this about the car industry?" I asked, dumbfounded.

"Don't forget, I just bought the ultimate boomer toy, my New Beetle. I did a bit of research before I took the plunge. It wasn't a simple matter of nostalgia on my part. Like you boomers, I pride myself on being a knowledgeable consumer," Ruth said smugly.

"So, O knowledgeable one, are you going to have dessert?" I asked as the waiter returned with the menu.

"I think I will. They have a great apple crisp here. Care to share an order?" she asked.

I nodded and the waiter headed back to the kitchen.

"Meredith," she continued, "I've done most of the talking today. I know you went to visit Sharon last week.

Do you want to talk about it?" she asked. "It must have been a tough week."

"That was the other thing that kept me awake last night. I was replaying the entire week in my head. Everything that happened to Sharon, everything we talked about. I guess I'm just sad about her condition. It's so unfair," I said, unable to continue.

"It's not unfair, unless you consider aging unfair," said Ruth quietly. "Deteriorating health is part and parcel of growing older."

"That's what frightens me," I replied. "I don't think I had any appreciation until now of how valuable a commodity health is."

"Health is the gift," remarked Ruth. "Health *care* is the commodity. And we're going to see its value rise significantly as boomers age. Back in 1991, approximately 12 percent of the Canadian population was over 65. By 2011 that figure will jump to over 14 percent. And, by 2031, over 20 percent of the population will be elderly. It's like that wise demographer Groucho Marx said many years ago: 'Anyone can get old. All you have to do is live long enough.' What we tend to overlook, however, is that many elderly Canadians are remarkably healthy and active living on their own. I'll tell you what worries me. The statistics show that we're seeing a marked increase in the number of single seniors — people living alone like me. I wonder, as families shrink in size, who will take care of us? But, I suppose it's like my uncle Jack always says, 'Better ten times ill than one time dead.' Right?"

"I suppose. But that's a pretty grim way of putting it," I answered.

"I guess I'm a bit afraid of the future, afraid of being alone. Our lives become meaningful when we are necessary to another person. I worry about becoming extraneous, unconnected." Ruth stared at me, and a bittersweet smile came over her face. I never imagined this woman feared anything, much less aging and loneliness! Life is truly filled with surprises.

12

Fad versus Trend: Theory

"Stratford must have been amazing. You still look like you're on vacation!" I said to a very relaxed looking Hazen when I reported to work on Tuesday morning.

"As I mentioned on Sunday, *A Man for All Seasons* was super. We all thought Brian Bedford stole the show in *Much Ado about Nothing*," he replied. "But the best part was spending time together as a family. I'd forgotten how well Dylan, Ruth and I get along, how much we like one another."

"A man for all seasons — sort of like you, Hazen. You're ready for anything the market has to dish out," I said.

"Being ready is all about anticipating where the market is headed," Hazen replied thoughtfully. "You know as well as I do, the market is not a perfectly predictable place. But that doesn't mean it's a crapshoot either. Like Peter Drucker says, if you're going to think about the future, focus on the things that have already happened — and will likely happen again. Demographics provides us with the framework to do just that, giving us with a window into the future. We know how many 15-year-olds will be living in Canada in 10 years because we know how many 5-year-olds we have here today."

"And the biggest bunch of all is the aging boomer generation," I said.

"My favourite topic," acknowledged Hazen. "And we can look at their past behaviour to predict — with some certainty, I believe — what they'll be doing in the future. A key to the accuracy of those predictions is the ability to discern between a fad and a trend. For successful long-term investing, the investor must be able to distinguish the difference between a trend, which will keep a company healthy for many years, and a fad, which will disappear as quickly as it arrived."

"How do you make that distinction?" I asked.

"Remember when the boom hit Hula Hoops and coonskin caps? If you recall how popular these fads once were, you will also remember how *unpopular* they became a short time later. Here, let me read you the definitions," he said, pulling a worn red dictionary off his bookshelf. "According to *Webster's*, a fad is short term in nature: 'a practice or interest followed for a time with exaggerated zeal.' A trend, on the other hand, sticks with us for many years: 'a prevailing tendency or inclination,' or 'a general movement.' Deciding whether events, businesses and products are short lived or here for the long term is a critical factor for successful long-term investing in financial markets."

"Give me an example I can understand," I challenged.

"Okay," replied Hazen slowly. I could almost see the gears working as he thought. "Elton John swept into Ottawa last winter. Eighteen thousand boomers shelled out $100 for tickets and another $30 for a babysitter. They packed the Corel Centre for a three-hour lovefest with the undisputed master of pop. Elton's career exemplifies the power of the boom, providing a perfect illustration of what can happen to a business enterprise — and Elton is nothing if not a business — that harnesses the power of the boom over the long term. Elton John, with a Top 40 single in *Billboard* every year since 1970, is a trend who markets straight into the hungry maw of the boom. If Elton John was publicly traded, you'd want a few shares of him in your portfolio."

"Pieter and I were at that concert — together with nearly every other boomer in Ottawa! So how does all of this play out in the real world?" I asked.

"As we've discussed before, the baby boom hits the market in two ways, directly and indirectly," Hazen answered. "At this moment, boomers are getting started at the process of affecting the stock market *indirectly*, investing their savings in mutual funds and individual stocks. Not only are boomers now in their prime earning years but they've also begun to prepare, in earnest, for their retirements. If you want to see proof of that, just look at the mutual fund industry. From 1990 to the end of 1997, assets under management by the Canadian mutual fund industry grew more than tenfold, making this the fastest-growing segment of the financial services market. But, in many ways, this is old news. We have been witnessing the power of this generation since boomers began arriving on the scene more than 50 years ago. Some commentators maintain that we are throwing off the stereotypes of the past, assuming personal identities that transcend the traditional boundaries of age, class and gender."

"I'd agree with that. I'd like to think that I'm a bit different from my parents," I said.

"Oh, you are, don't worry. However, when it gets right down to the basics, each of us still needs to eat, work and find a place to hang our hat. It's at this basic level that we see the immense power of the boom," replied Hazen. "After they crowded through the school system, boomers muscled into the world of work. That meant finding a place to live and furnishing it. To do that, the boomers borrowed — big time. Along the way, they pushed up the price of real estate and sent interest rates into double digits during the 1980s. Now that they're settled, it's no surprise to see interest rates returning to traditional levels and housing prices coming back to earth. That leaves stocks and bonds as the investment vehicle of choice. Back in the 1950s and '60s, people opted to keep approximately 40 to 45 percent of their wealth invested in stocks and bonds. That investing strategy fell into disfavour in the 1970s and '80s. At that time, with interest rates and real estate prices soaring courtesy of boomers just entering their adult years and forming new households, holdings of stocks and bonds fell back to approximately 20 percent of household wealth. Unlike their parents, however, boomers can't rely on GICs and real estate to provide them with a comfortable retirement. Not surprisingly, we're watching a return to equity markets during the 1990s."

"But the boomers have been affecting the markets directly throughout their lives," I stated.

"And it's that direct impact of the boom that you're going to be researching for me over the next couple of weeks," Hazen said. "Along the length of the baby boom, many companies have sold into the power of this massive generation. Some have been fads while others have achieved trend status. Like Elton John, McDonald's is a trend. In fact, with nearly 24,000 restaurants in over 110 countries, McDonald's has created its own global village. The company has a history of combining solid management with a strong respect for and understanding of the needs and wants of the boomers. Back in the 1960s, it catered to the appetites of hungry teenagers and families filled with young boomer kids who wanted cheap food and lots of it. Now, with its offerings of adult products and toys for the children of time-crunched parents, it continues to meet the wants of families headed by middle-aged boomers. To maintain trend status, companies that serve the boom must keep on top of where this generation is right now and where it's headed next."

"Is McDonald's up to the challenge?"

"If you look at the demographic statistics, there aren't as many young children coming along to become McDonald's devotees," Hazen responded. "There are 400,000 four-year-olds in Canada. That number declines steadily the younger you go, moving down to somewhere around 360,000 newborns. If that keeps up, McDonald's will find itself marketing into a shrinking group of children."

"I think you're right on that score. There was a time when we couldn't drive past a McDonald's without the kids begging to eat there. Now Malcolm turns his nose up at a Big Mac, saying he'd rather go to Harvey's instead. McDonald's will have to reinvent itself to reclaim the boomers once they're out of child-rearing mode," I said.

"Just like McDonald's, all companies must watch the boom — or ignore it at their peril. Look at the business of athletic shoes, for example. In the American imagination, athletic shoes have surpassed trend status to achieve an iconic level in the marketplace. 'Just Do It' became the mantra of billions of consumers, pushing athletic shoes to the top of the heap, where they account for the largest share of shoes sold today. But that trend is showing signs of slowing from a rampage to a trickle. The athletic shoe share of the footwear market tumbled significantly during the 1990s."

"Maybe it's time for those companies to pay attention to the boomers," I said.

"Good point," said Hazen with a smile. "Typically, manufacturers have focused their marketing on teens and young adults. Sounds logical — these are the people who are most physically active, right? But a closer look reveals that a lowly 19 percent of athletic shoes are bought for exercise purposes. The rest are purchased by those of us who want a comfortable shoe for our aging feet. Perhaps Nike's recent slide wouldn't have been as dramatic if the company had spent some time analyzing the boomers. For years, Nike has been at the top of this fast-paced business, targeting its marketing straight into the world of active teenage boys and young men. Nike is still at the top of the heap, but it recently watched sales drop like a stone. In 1998, worldwide orders decreased by 13 percent. A number of factors conspired to precipitate this decline, including better competition and the onset of economic woes in Asia. But that slide also has something to do with misdirected marketing. Even Nike CEO Philip Knight acknowledged that the company must do something to reignite excitement in the U.S. market for Nike products."

"I bet they ignored the power of the boom," I said.

"Right again," said Hazen. "Teenage boys do buy athletic shoes, but it's the baby boomers who pack the real purchasing power in this country. And Nike is showing signs of waking up to that fact. They're replacing the aggressive 'Just Do It' tag line with the kinder, gentler 'I Can.' Now, that's more appealing to an aging boomer with creaky bones. Plus — an interesting aside — Nike is paying close attention to the global demographics of the wider world around it. Populations of Third World countries are rising faster than those of wealthier nations, and the sport of choice in many of those countries is soccer. So it should come as no surprise that a fleet-footed Nike is running headlong into the soccer shoe market. The company's new goal is to be the world leader in soccer by 2002, the year of the next World Cup. The company is busy assembling partnerships with U.S. Soccer and top European club teams. Amazing when you consider that Nike was barely in the soccer market five years ago."

"Courtesy of our research into global demographics, I now know that there are nearly six billion people around the world," I said. "Ignore the world at your peril. Maybe there's hope for Nike."

"Here's another example," said Hazen. "Mackenzie Financial Corp., distributor of more than 50 mutual funds, is a company that has always kept the baby boomers in clear sight. By cashing in on a major boomer trend — the desire to prepare for retirement — Mackenzie and companies like it have become a trend in their own right. Offering a wide range of mutual funds — the current investment vehicle of choice for the boomers — the company administers more than $30 billion worth of assets, making it one of the top five mutual fund companies in Canada. So, how does this company plan to maintain its trend status? Keep watching the boomers mature. The boomers are just beginning to invest in financial markets and they're looking to mutual fund managers for basic advice. But it's not always going to be that way. As the boom ages and becomes more experienced in the ways of financial markets, many will become capable of investing directly in the market. How will Mackenzie position itself to sell to these more sophisticated investors? By offering products with strong growth potential that boomers don't know much about. Mackenzie is currently positioning itself for the inheritance windfall that will be coming to the boomers over the next decade as their parents die. The company sees a time when mass-marketing of mutual funds won't be enough for many boomers. These boomers, interested in investing their own nest egg plus whatever they have inherited, will want Mackenzie to deliver a more customized product, tailored to their individual needs. Mackenzie is now putting the technology in place to allow it to deliver those portfolio management services."

"So how can the average investor tell the difference between a fad and a trend stock?" I asked.

"Funny you should ask. One of the things that I've been working on is a framework of 10 elements that help identify a long-term trend. This framework — a sort of user guide — can help investors separate long-term trends from short-term fads, help them identify companies that are riding trends for the long term as opposed to businesses that are selling fads over the short haul. And I want you to work with that framework over the next couple of weeks, searching out companies that fit into the trend framework, companies that will be positively affected by the boom. But I also want a few examples of companies that fall outside of my framework — fad stocks. In my presentation, I want to be able to provide some solid examples of companies that stand to benefit from the power of the boom and some that have lost sight of the gigantic generation."

"Can I take a look at this framework?" I asked.

"Certainly. I've made a copy for you to use during your research." Hazen picked up a sheet of paper from his desk and handed it to me.

"Thanks," I said, slipping on my glasses to read Hazen's trademark tidy handwriting. This is what I read:

1. Duration — Are the boomers in it for a short time or do they stay? Preparing for their retirements, boomers will be using financial services for a long time to come. How long can aging boomers (and their bones) keep on rollerblading?
2. Frequency — Do boomers do it regularly or seldom? (Avoid snide comments here!) If they don't do it very often, it better be expensive.
3. Flexibility — Can the company keep up with what's happening in society? Specifically, can it keep up with the boomers? Look at how Bombardier has transformed its business, moving from snowmobiles into the high-profit world of commuter planes that keep busy boomer commuters out of overcrowded hub airports.
4. Quantity — Will sales of the company's products increase as boomers age? Do the boomers want more or less of the product as they grow older? If McDonald's doesn't watch out, boomers will be consuming less of their product as they age. Estée Lauder markets its high-quality cosmetics to boomer women, playing on their concerns about aging skin — a guarantee of increasing sales.
5. Quantity — If the boomers don't want more of the product, do they want a higher quality — and more expensive versions — of the product? Think cars. When they were young, boomers drove cheap little Toyota Corollas. Now they're cruising town in their pricey Lexus sedans, the high-end Toyota line. Boomers are willing to pay more for those Toyota products as they age.

6. Gender-Bending — Does the company market to both sexes? The cosmetics industry has expanded its reach to aging boomer men, concerned with keeping their youthful looks. Smart!
7. Cross-Generations — While there's no denying the power of the boom, the clever company tries to capture the imagination of the entire population, reaching the biggest market possible. Adaptability is the key here. Think of the Gap. Although the accessories are definitely going to be different, a classic pair of khakis can appeal as equally to a boomer banker in Sarnia as a teenage girl in Sudbury. The cruise industry is also working hard these days at changing cruises from a retiree's dream to the fantasy of every vacationer.
8. Mega-Trends — Is the company able to identify the larger trends in society? On the flipside, can the company distinguish between a true trend and the trimmings of a trend? There's a move towards a more casual way of life — think casual Fridays, for example. That's a mega-trend. The smart clothing company will recognize this trend, selling products that reflect this less formal approach to dressing for work.
9. Availability — Where can I buy the thing? The goal — everywhere! Look at ubiquitous companies like Wal-Mart, Loblaws, Canadian Tire, Sears. Being everywhere for everyone is a great start on the road to trend status.
10. Benefits — Does it deliver to the boomers? Boomers have dragged us into the pressure-cooker era of the time crunch. The catalogue business — companies

like Lands' End, Siegel, L.L. Bean — has effectively tapped into and profited from that pressure by providing a service that allows boomers to shop at any time of the day or night, alleviating their crushing time deficit.

"Now, what I want you to do," said Hazen once I'd finished reading his list, "is to research the companies I've mentioned in this list and add some new ones. You know my focus is always on large, reputable blue-chip companies. I'd like a couple of ideas and companies from each criterion on the list in order to give investors an idea of the characteristics they should be looking for in companies to include for their investment portfolios. Finally, don't worry if some of your suggestions overlap with companies we've already examined in the course of our research — it shows that those companies are really tuned in to the demographics of the world around them."

I had my instructions — I was off to seek trends.

13

Fad versus Trend: Applied

"I could help you with your work, Mom," said Emily. We were finishing up our dinner, over which I had been telling Pieter and the kids that Hazen had asked me to spend the next couple of weeks identifying fads and trends in the business world.

"What's your idea, sweetheart?" I asked, thinking "out of the mouths of babes . . ." In fact, the kids had been very helpful over the summer months. Our family seemed to have arrived at a happy compromise — the kids were thriving on a mix of responsibility and freedom. Malcolm was responsible for delivering Emily to her day camp at Carleton University each morning, then he travelled by bus to the downtown Y for a leader-in-training program. Their helpfulness was a great relief after a tough spring with my son. Raising kids was like anything else, I thought: if you could make it through the down periods, you'd live to see — and enjoy — the upside.

"Well, like, you know how I like the Spice Girls but you don't?" she asked, interrupting my reverie.

"They're not my favourite group," I acknowledged, wondering where her logic was taking her.

"But then, like, you know how we both like Sarah McLachlan? How you and me are going to see her at Lilith Fair later this month?" she asked.

I nodded.

"So," Emily continued slowly, "Spice Girls are a fad because only girls my age like them, but everybody — even Dad and Malcolm — likes Sarah McLachlan. So Sarah is a trend. Do you get it? The more people that like you and buy your CDs, that's what makes you a trend. People of all ages like Sarah. And they're going to like her for a long time."

I stared at her in amazement. "That's exactly right," I exclaimed. "In fact, that's one of the criteria that Hazen has identified as marking a trend — the cross-generational appeal of the product. In other words, that people of all ages like and use the product. Good thinking, Emily! Things haven't changed much since I was a little girl. In my day we had the Monkees and the Beatles. The Monkees were the fad and the Beatles were the trend. Even you still listen to them. You know, it pays to play your own instrument and write your own songs — the Beatles did that and Sarah is still doing it!" We shared a smile.

"Here's what I think," she continued. "The Spice Girls should have listened to one of their own songs. It's called

'Stop.' There's a line that goes, 'Racing so hard you know it won't last.' That's the Spice Girls. But then there's another line in the same song: 'Slow down, read the signs, so you know just where you're going.' That's Sarah McLachlan."

I watched her finish clearing dishes off the table. She'd hit the nail on the head. Hazen was trying to teach investors to distinguish between the tidal wave of a fad and the slow, steady building of a trend. Hazen's approach was "slow down, read the signs," always focusing on the fundamentals. He advised investors first and foremost to focus their investment strategy on blue-chip stocks, the shares of large, reputable companies. These stocks tend to be lower risk than those of smaller growth companies. Then, he instructed investors to determine whether the company has a viable, long-term plan in place. A key to that long-term plan is knowing who your customers will be in the future. That's where demographics comes in, telling companies how many, how old, where and who their customers will be as their long-term plan unfolds into the future. A critical part of focusing on the fundamentals? Paying attention to demographics. And that's what Hazen's fad-versus-trend work was all about — paying attention.

I spent the next two weeks combing the Net and snooping around the library. I filled in Hazen's fad-versus-trend framework, finding one or two companies or sectors that fit into each of his 10 criteria.

Here's what I produced:

(1) Duration — Two simple words: health care. It's been called the growth sector of the future. And boomers are going to be in it for a good, long time. The boomers are aging, and with age come health issues. Look at recent breast cancer statistics. Breast cancer is a leading form of cancer diagnosed in Canadian women — approximately one woman in nine can expect to develop the disease.

Plenty of people are concerned that breast cancer seems to be more common than ever among women aged 40 to 49. In fact, according to Statistics Canada, the expanding numbers of new cases can be accounted for by the aging of the baby boomers. When the growing number of boomer women moving into this age range is taken into consideration, the incidence rates for breast cancer have remained stable for younger women. According to StatsCan, the incidence rate is approximately 130 per 100,000 women aged 40 to 49.

What is different, however, is that mortality rates — deaths due to breast cancer — are declining. By mid-1990, the mortality rate was at the lowest it's been since 1950. These impressive declines come from a couple of sources: earlier detection of tumours and more effective treatments.

MDS Nordion is one of the companies that's at the leading edge both diagnosing and treating breast cancer. This company is developing products such as radio-labelled tumour markers, which help detect difficult-to-spot tumours. MDS Nordion is also a leading manufacturer of radiation therapy equipment used to treat cancers, including breast cancer. This company, with 6,800 employees, is in for the long haul, focused on preventing, diagnosing and managing disease — very important in a world where more and more people are placing demands on the health care system. Doctors and hospitals are becoming busier with all manner of health care concerns. In Ontario alone, patient visit volumes have increased significantly — up 12 percent each year.

In these days of keeping costs in check, the goal is to keep the patient out of hospital. Pfizer Pharmaceuticals, best known as the maker of Viagra, has made reducing the cost of disease one of its main corporate goals. Economists agree with this approach, suggesting that countries that spend more on pharmaceuticals not only achieve longer life expectancy but also are associated with fewer and shorter hospital admissions.

Companies specializing in private home care stand to cash in on the aging boomers. In fact, this trend is well under way. In the Ottawa region, some 12 percent of all new businesses started in 1997 offered health care products or services, up from virtually none a couple of years before. As the health care system cuts back on hospital stays while boomers place more demands on it, more and more people will need home care services, including nursing help and nutritional and stress counselling, for example. Investors need to show some caution here and not lose sight of the actual age of the boomers — they might be *aging* but they're far from old. Boomers might need physiotherapy services, but they're not yet ready for nursing homes.

Combine boomer aging and longer life expectancies and we'll be looking at health care for the duration!

What will boomers be leaving behind them as they age? Toy purchases, for one. As their children age and as the number of babies entering the economy dwindles, the toy business will be in for a tough time — unless it adapts. Keep a careful eye on a company like Toys "R" Us, Inc. It's already closed nearly 60 stores. As other toy retailers have successfully moved into educational, computer-based toys, Toys "R" Us has faithfully stuck by Barbie and her ilk. Problem is, the boomers' kids have outgrown Barbie. Can Toys "R" Us grow with the boomers' children? Does it realize that the next generation to produce kids is some 30 percent smaller than the boomers?

(2) Frequency — If it's cheap, people better use it often. The sector that leaps to mind is information and communications technology. Huge amounts of money have been invested by many companies in this sector. We've seen costs go down. Remember how much mobile phones used to cost? Now they're giving them away as part of a service package. The flipside? When they were introduced, mobile phones were the domain of the wealthy. Go into any high school today and you'll find teenagers chatting on their cells, financed by their babysitting jobs! It's all about access — which has increased exponentially.

Now, if you want to talk about frequency, talk about the future of television viewing in this country. In 1952, when CBC first hit the airwaves, there were only 146,000 television sets in the entire country. Now television watching is our dominant leisure activity. And the statistics show that the hours spent watching TV increase as we age. Men aged 35 to 49 spend fewer than 20 hours each week in front of the boob tube. That number goes up dramatically for men 60 and over — they watch more than 30 hours of television. This bodes well for the television industry as the boomers age. CanWest Global Communications Corp., this country's most profitable private-sector television broadcaster, has positioned itself well, understanding the plugged-in, tuned-in future that lies ahead for many boomers. This company owns and operates the Global television and cable networks. It's just become a national force with the recent acquisition of Alberta-based WIC, Western International Communications Ltd., allowing it to expand coverage to nearly 90 percent of Canada's English-speaking population — some 11 million households. That's plenty of TV watching!

What about those products that aren't used all that often? Those things had better be pretty pricey. Intrawest Corp. is an example of a company that markets a product — downhill skiing — that is not used every day by everyone in society. And yet Intrawest is a very successful Canadian company. By marketing an upscale experience, with quaint villages filled with restaurants and shops, they've made consumers happy to part with upwards of $50 a day for the privilege of skiing on their hills. They're not just selling a product, they're selling an experience. And that experience allows them to charge more for their services.

Of course, the ultimate example of the high-priced product is the family home. We've usually got only one at a time. We don't go out to buy one very often and we're doing it even less as we age. Plus, the market for new housing shows signs of dwindling as the smaller generations following the boomers move into their home-buying years.

(3) Flexibility — Keep up with society — and what it wants. Sounds easy, but many companies have foundered trying to figure out where society — the baby-boom generation in particular — is headed. Look at Levi's. This company, which produced the uniform of young boomers, is looking as worn and tattered as a pair of its jeans. Levi's recently closed four factories in Europe and 10 sewing plants in the U.S. It's been eclipsed by younger companies like Tommy Hilfiger and the Gap. Levi's became known as "the jeans my dad wears," the kiss of death for a product that must capture the youth market if it hopes to prosper. And the youth market — the echo generation — is a large (some seven million strong) wealthy group in this country. The company is making a stab at getting back into the game with its line of "Hard Jeans," rigid, cuffed jeans made from hard, dark, unwashed denim. It remains to be seen whether Levi's can hold on to its title as the world's largest branded apparel manufacturer by promising to sell uncomfortable pants.

Disney, on the other hand, has shown itself to be eminently — and creatively — flexible over the years. This company has long been the jewel in the crown of the echo boom market. It's into everything that children and teens consume — animated movies, toys, theme parks, clothing, television, you name it. In fact, if an investor had purchased one Disney share back in 1955 for $34 and held on for the ride, that holding would be worth at least $20,000 in September 1997. The key to their success? They continue to mature along with the echo boom and their boomer parents. At their theme parks, for example, they've kept Mickey and Minnie but added General Motors' test track, a hot draw for older teenagers. The company now dominates television coverage of U.S. football. Not only is Disney continuing to make movies for kids — *Mulan* and *Pocahontas* are two recent examples — they're dominating the adult movie market too. Did you know that the mega-success *The English Patient* is a Disney movie? The company is also keeping on top of today's families by sailing into the cruise industry with the *Disney Magic*, a ship the size of an aircraft carrier that can carry 2,400 passengers. In the 2000s, Disney stands to benefit enormously from the re-release of its vast film library, feeding on the nostalgia of the boomers craving to relive the experiences of their childhoods.

Like Intrawest, Disney is fully aware that it is selling memorable experiences, not mere services. And those experiences, wrapped around a service like a cruise or a movie or a hotel room, can command a higher-than-average fee when staged by the pioneers in the experience economy.

(4) Quantity — In the 1980s, boomer women were aging, they were rapidly entering the workforce *and* they wanted to keep themselves looking good. The Estée Lauder Companies recognized that cluster of changes and marketed straight into it, leading to the first billion-dollar sales quarter in its history. Estée Lauder markets its high-quality products to boomer women, playing on their concerns about aging skin and desire that makeup

be easy and quick to use. The company knows that as they age, boomer women will be using more, rather than less, makeup. Estée Lauder is also keeping a close eye on demographics in the big world, selling its well-recognized products in more than 100 countries and territories.

But Estée Lauder isn't the only cosmetic company looking across borders for its future success. Avon Products, Inc. has operations in 45 countries and, unlike many other companies who are just starting to "go global," it has been doing business overseas for more than 40 years. Avon sells to women in 135 countries through its network of 2.6 million sales representatives. That network of mainly women is what will carry Avon successfully into the future. As Louise Yamada asks us, why wouldn't a Chinese woman want to earn $1,000 a month selling Avon products instead of $100 for factory work? Finally, "never underestimate the vanity of woman, and now even man," advises Yamada.

Now, if you want to see an old reliable quantity company that just keeps on truckin', look at Canadian Tire. It's the source most Canadians turn to when they need antifreeze, fishing rods or a new light fixture. Cars, cottages and homes — three major preoccupations of many Canadians and three things that generate many purchases. With its 430 stores and revenues of well over $4 billion per year, Canadian Tire is a home away from home for all of these products.

(5) Quality — If there's one thing we've got plenty of these days, it's information. Courtesy of the Internet, television and telephone, data moves around the planet instantaneously and cheaply. But data is one thing;

interpreting and using that vast quantity of data is something quite different. That's why Merrill Lynch's long-term strategy makes solid good sense. Merrill Lynch is positioning itself as a "wisdom company." "Our role," explains vice-chairman John Steffens, "is to sort through all the information in this complex world and translate it into wisdom our clients can use."

It appears that the financial services industry — Merrill Lynch is one of its largest members — is in the process of dividing into two segments. One segment will be "do-it-yourself" companies, such as discount brokers, who give their customers plenty of information and the opportunity to invest in the markets. The Toronto-Dominion Bank through its discount brokerage, TD Green Line, is a good example of this type of company. In advertising to consumers, they emphasize savings, specifically reduced commission charges. These are the "quantity" companies. The second type of company adopts a different approach. Looking at the time crunch and information overload that most boomers are suffering, these companies, including Merrill Lynch, focus on developing a personal advisory relationship with their clients. These are the "quality" companies.

Merrill Lynch is convinced it is on the right track, pointing out that investors with advice do better than those without — they tend to buy their investments earlier in the market cycle and hold them longer. In addition, investors with advisers tend to hold on to their shares during downturns in the market and, as any reformed market timer can tell you, time in the market is more valuable than timing the market.

If you think about the progression of the boomers, they tend to move from quantity to quality — if they can afford it. Moving to more expensive homes, acquiring more upscale clothing, consuming higher-priced foods, buying more personal services. Merrill Lynch is betting on boomers — time crunched, overloaded and full of anxiety for the well-being of their retirement funds — to lead them into the next millennium.

Loblaw Cos. Ltd. is building its future on the same boomer traits. It too has decided to focus on delivering quality to its customers. With its house brand, President's Choice, Loblaws offers easy-to-prepare foods that might be more expensive than other products but compare in quality to the premium name brands. But President's Choice products are less expensive than those premium name brands. Quality plus ease of preparation, at cheaper prices — that sounds like a recipe boomers will approve of, keeping Loblaws in the top position among Canadian food retailers with over 20 percent of the market.

And boomers are looking for "only the very best" for their kids too. Montreal-based Cinar Films Inc. has cleverly identified this trend. Cinar develops and produces non-violent, high-quality programming and educational products for children. If you have a young child, you've seen their stuff — *Arthur*, *Emily of New Moon*, *Lassie*. Now let's see if this company knows how to grow with their media-savvy audiences.

(6) Gender-Bending — Long ago and far away, the computer geek stereotype was always male — wearing glasses, pens in a shirt pocket protector and a calculator

hooked to his belt. Toss that stereotype! Computers and related technology have changed the way we work, the way we think, the way we play, the way we communicate, the way we shop — just about everything. That means computers are no longer the domain of geeks and, more important, no longer the domain of males. A recent survey found that women account for nearly 50 percent of "connected" people (they use e-mail at least three days a week and use three of the following regularly: a laptop, a cell phone, a beeper and a home computer). Now, think how that has expanded the market for products and services that were once a male preserve!

Two companies stand at the ready, prepared to use the newest technologies to deliver to eager consumers. Canada's leading hi-tech company, Northern Telecom Ltd. — Nortel — is a telecommunications equipment developer and manufacturer, homing in on both the wireline and wireless telecom markets. With its recent acquisition of Bay Networks, Nortel is ready to integrate the Internet into its networking products, moving the company ahead into the race to "stay connected."

Then there's the American behemoth, America Online. This Internet company calls itself the global leader in "interactive services." What does this mean? It's an Internet online provider — the world's largest, with 13 million subscribers. AOL provides e-mail and chat services. Members go to AOL for their news, to send photos to family members, to check the stock markets and — maybe most crucial — to buy stuff. As Internet technology matures, becoming easier to use and attracting more and more users, AOL is bracing itself for the onslaught of the mass market coming online.

(7) Cross-Generations — Think of a company like the Gap. With its simple, well-designed casual clothing sold at popular prices, it has pulled in not only boomer parents but also their children. It's no surprise that the company now operates more than 2,000 stores. Like Nike, however, the Gap has had its missteps along the way — blips when the big spenders on clothing, the boomers, were ignored. Their 1997 line — tiny tops and mini-miniskirts — catered to the kids crowd. Take a walk through the Gap today and you'll see classic shirts and comfortable pants appealing across the generation gap.

Nostalgia is a great marketing tool to pull in all generations of our society. Look at the outpouring in the summer of 1998 when boomer TV favourites Roy Rogers, Buffalo Bob and Shari Lewis all hung up their spurs. Not only were these three staples in the daily viewing diet of the young boomers, they became well known to the generations that followed. Lamb Chop, Shari Lewis's sidekick, was just as popular with echo kids as she had been with little boomers who watched TV sprawled on the rec-room floor lo those many years ago — a definite trend. Boomers want to remember those carefree days of their childhoods, and young generations find the "niceness" of nostalgia appealing too. Remember, boomers might be seeing Roy Rogers for the second time, but he's a fresh face to the children of the boomers.

More than a few companies have jumped on the nostalgia bandwagon. Denny's restaurants is a good example. This company has recently introduced a new chain of

'50s- and '60s-style eatery, Denny's Classic Diner, in the hopes of cashing in on the wave of nostalgia sweeping North America as the boomers age. Wendy's is getting in on the game too with its newest offering, Wendy's Old Fashioned Hamburger Restaurants.

Then there are the cinema wars. For the next couple of years we're going to be watching Cineplex Odeon and Famous Players duke it out over the Canadian movie-going audience. Both companies know that the movie business covers all generations — the boomers no longer have babies to tend, freeing up an evening or two for the cinema, and the echo kids are now old enough to hit the movies on their own. We're back into the era of colossal and very grand movie palaces (some of these theatres can seat nearly 4,000), designed to appeal to mom, dad, the kids and their grandparents too!

(8) Mega-Trends — The boomers have dragged us into the era of the time crunch. Nearly 60 percent of young families in which both parents work outside the home feel trapped in a time pressure cooker. The time crunch is a boomer mega-trend. Take a look at how the catalogue business has profited from that pressure: five years ago, 42 percent of Americans had bought from a catalogue. Now that number stands at 52 percent. Why? Catalogue shopping is convenient, it's easy and, because you can do it at any time of the day or night, it alleviates that crushing time deficit. One catalogue company that's ridden this trend is Lands' End. From its beginnings in 1963 selling sailboat hardware, it moved into the clothing market, retailing traditionally styled casual clothing for men, women and children. Last year sales exceeded

$1 billion. And this company knows its demographics. It knows that the majority of its shoppers are working women, ranging in age from 35 to 54. Sound like a familiar group? Orders can be placed 24 hours a day, 364 days a year; Christmas is the only day their phone lines are closed. Here's what Lands' End delivers to its shoppers: clothes and time.

Okay, we all want to be in better physical shape and look better, right? Fighting age — that's a boomer trend. Who is taking advantage of this trend? Golf is definitely on the upswing with aging boomers and their children, the populous echo generation. A company like Callaway Golf Co., a well-established manufacturer of golf equipment, is well positioned to capitalize on the boomers' desire to keep fit. In Canada, Ontario-based Clublink is combining the boomers' desire for a stress-free vacation and newfound love of golf by acquiring a string of favourite Muskoka resorts and golf courses.

Then there are the look-good-feel-good companies that produce health care products. As boomers' eyesight fails, there's Johnson & Johnson, the leading producer of disposable contact lenses. Not surprisingly, the company is watching sales of its skin care products increase — got to keep those wrinkles in check! And pain relievers are selling better than ever — oh, my aching bones!

(9) Availability — We can sum this up in one word: Wal-Mart. Here's what Wal-Mart knows: because of improved manufacturing technologies, production costs are about as low as they can now go. So where's the profit going to come from? A retailer like Wal-Mart can give consumers a better deal (and themselves a higher profit margin) if it

can bring down distribution costs and service costs and sell vast quantities of product. And that's just what Wal-Mart has done. Last year, Wal-Mart, with the help of its nearly one million employees (or associates, as it likes to call them), racked up exceptionally impressive earnings growth of 15 percent. They're everywhere!

They're everywhere and they're usually in a hurry. Companies like Lenscrafters have figured this out. They know that some 80 percent of the population over the age of 40 needs some sort of assistance with their vision — glasses or contacts, for example. They also know that these weak-sighted boomers are short for time. So Lenscrafters has built its business on servicing customers within an hour. Laser eye surgery companies like TLC The Laser Centre are betting that aging boomers will opt for surgery rather than glasses; these companies hope this corrective alternative will become the most widely performed surgical procedure worldwide by the year 2000.

Keep sight of other developing trends that are everywhere. The Internet has the potential to be (and to sell) all things to all people, especially boomers. Companies like Amazon.com and now Chapters are endeavouring to get boomers buying books online, offering tremendous selection, easy access and bargain-basement prices.

(10) Benefits — A company that provides plenty of benefits to the consumer is definitely on the right track. Many individual entrepreneurs stand to gain from the boomers' desire for services. Boomers are going to be looking for help to cater their parties, clean their houses, shop for their cars. It's estimated that this market tallies $15 bil-

lion in Canada. On a larger scale, Sears is striving to be a pre-eminent provider of services. Of course, they still produce their famous catalogue — boomers can definitely appreciate the advantages of catalogue shopping, as already mentioned. But there's more. Sears wants to own the home service sector in this country. It wants not only to install your carpet and dishwasher but also to shovel your driveway, wash your kitchen floors and redecorate your family room. Sears recently opened 16 Whole Home Furniture stores, which offer a 24-hour phone line allowing homeowners to book workers to service their needs.

Look at Bombardier. It's busy providing benefits of a different sort. Bombardier manufactures planes, trains and subway systems, to name a few of its products. Although this company is headquartered in Canada, it has a global presence. You've seen its products if you've ridden the monorail through Walt Disney World in Florida. Think about Bombardier's recent big sales of its commuter planes — a whopping $627 million was added to its order book in 1997. Bombardier is focusing on aircraft that profitably service "thin" routes, the routes that keep travellers out of overcrowded hub airports like Atlanta and Chicago. And this company's good news just keeps on going. It inked a $2-billion deal with the Virgin Rail Group of the United Kingdom to supply and maintain rolling stock, including the design of 36 locomotives and 140 coaches. As boomers age and spend more time travelling, Bombardier is perfectly positioned for growth.

I presented this list together with a file of information concerning each company to Hazen at his home on a Friday in the middle of August — I had to finish my presentation early because Emily and I were off in the late afternoon to see our favourite trend, Sarah McLachlan. Lilith Fair had rolled into Ottawa! To my great relief, Hazen was very pleased with my "trendsetting" work.

"This is a great list," he stated. "Very understandable and accessible. In my seminar, I don't really want to give my listeners a list of companies to invest in. What I want to do is to give them the skills to figure out for themselves the types of companies that stand to benefit from the boomers. As the boomers hit their peak spending years, the issue of discerning between a fad and a trend continues to be a key consideration for investors."

"From the research I did for this list, it certainly appears that the successful investors will be those who are able to identify the telltale signs and purchase stocks accordingly," I added. "Trends do pay off."

"But," said Hazen steadily, "I want to remind my audience that although demographics provide a valuable tool for identifying investments, they're not the only tool. Investors must factor other fundamental information about a company into their investment decisions."

"Like what?" I asked.

"Well, let's look at an example," continued Hazen. "The Loewen Group, a B.C.-based funeral home company, was founded by Ray Loewen after he spent his childhood working in the family funeral home. During the late '80s and early '90s, the Loewen Group was in exponential growth mode. Ray Loewen built the company into North

America's second-largest funeral services company, with more than 1,000 funeral homes and 500 cemeteries. Now it looks as if this company is in serious trouble. That phenomenal growth — specifically the focus on growth to the exclusion of everything else — may be what brought the high-flying company down. Loewen Group paid more than its competitors did for all those funeral homes. That kept its debt levels high compared with those of its competitors. The company also found itself embroiled in a U.S. lawsuit that ended up costing nearly $200 million. Its management system was renowned for being decentralized — difficult in a company trying to manage so many different funeral homes. Finally, Loewen Group's long-term strategy of pre-selling cemetery plots never met projections. Boomers aren't into that market quite yet. They know they're aging but they're not prepared to face death!"

"Okay," I said, "here's what your Loewen Group example tells me. In addition to demographics, investors should keep an eye on the quality of management, levels of sales and earnings, long-term business strategies and management systems."

"You got it," replied Hazen, glancing down at his watch. "It's nearly three. Shouldn't you be going?"

"Thanks for letting me off early," I said, stacking my files of company information on his desk. "You should tell your audience that the Internet is a great way to find out about individual companies. Not only do the companies have their own home pages where they speak directly about strategies regarding demographics, but you can also find great commentary on those firms —

newspaper articles, for example." As I began gathering my things to leave, Dylan appeared at the door.

"We didn't hear you come in," said a surprised Hazen.

Dylan laughed. "I let myself in the back door. I live here, remember? I wanted to tell you both my good news. Dad, you're going to be proud of me. I've come home with not just one but two jobs. And one of my jobs is actually in my field of study!"

"So, do tell," said his father.

"On the way home I was thinking that I'm really tapping in to the boomer market with both of them," said Dylan. "During the week, I'm going to be tutoring children in math at a small new private school over on Fisher Avenue. And on Friday and Saturday nights, I'll be waiting tables at that new diner on Bank Street. I'll be teaching the boomers' kids on weekdays and feeding the boomers and those same kids on weekends! Great, eh?"

"There you go, Hazen," I said, smiling at him. "Your very own son fits into your trend framework — he's providing benefits to a success-driven, nostalgic cross-generational crowd."

"Pardon me?" queried Dylan.

"Ask your dad. I'm off to my own trend," I said, closing the door on father and son.

14

Lions, Tigers and Bears – Oh No!

Lilith Fair was a great start to our weekend. And I couldn't wait to tell Hazen about the crowd that packed into Lansdowne Park for the event — plenty of boomers, lots with kids in tow like me, many twentysomethings, a horde of very hip looking teenagers. (How come today's teenagers look so much more together than we did at that age?) I decided that Sarah McLachlan fit squarely into Hazen's cross-generations criterion on his trend framework.

On Saturday, Pieter and I strolled over to Frank and Jean Wallace's home. Since the day Hazen and I met with Francis, I'd been thinking about the Wallace house, imagining my family living in it, mentally redecorating the living room with our furniture. I was becoming like Pieter — I needed more in my life than a rental home,

I needed a place that I could make my own, somewhere to put down some lasting roots.

Pieter saw the potential in the house immediately. All around it, the houses had been extensively renovated with family rooms tucked on the back, new windows, fancy landscaping and the like. The Wallace house stood in their midst, extremely well maintained, but in its original condition. I watched the wheels clicking in Pieter's brain. He's really a frustrated builder, and I could see he was itching to get his hands on that house. We spent the weekend talking about our desire to make a family place for our kids, our plans for the long run, our commitment to our neighbourhood, its schools and people. And we talked about our finances. Since moving to the Glebe, we'd straightened ourselves out. Our debts were manageable, our savings regular, we had committed ourselves to a long-term investment plan. In fact, our RRSPs, courtesy of the stocks we'd purchased, had shown real growth over the past couple of years. We were actually starting to feel back on track. We decided that if the Wallace house was priced within our range, we'd make an offer.

And then came Monday. The news was filled with the story. Russia's economy came to a crashing halt on Monday, August 17 — the banking system collapsed, the ruble lost more than half its value. The television coverage was brutal — people fighting to get into banks to withdraw their life savings, all too reminiscent of the beginning of the Great Depression in North America. And then the contagion started to spread. That week, we started to hear more about the financial crisis in Asia,

Latin America — Brazil, in particular. By the end of the week, there was talk of a recession in North America. The global economy meant that bad news overseas was certain to make its way here. And, of course, stock markets around the world were pummelled by all this bad news. Commentators were talking about the "swan dive" performed by North American markets. The Dow Jones industrial average and the TSE were both posting percentage drops the likes of which hadn't been seen in a long time.

And, all the while, I watched our wealth drain away — $1,000 one day, $550 the next. It was pretty scary! Hazen was out of town on business for the week, so I was left to stew in my own juices for a few days. Pieter was preoccupied with work and unperturbed by the events around him. The entire experience was too reminiscent of our first foray into the real estate market — and the big losses we incurred when we sold our suburban monster home. By Friday, I had convinced myself that the markets were on the verge of melting down, taking our life savings with them.

The final straw was laid across my back that Friday evening. I was standing in the checkout line at the grocery store when the tabloid caught my eye. "Wall Street Bloodbath!" its front page screamed. "2nd Great Depression Is Just Weeks Away!" Now, I had always considered the tabloid press, with its seamy coverage of Monica Lewinsky and other media stars, to be lower than low. But this — this prediction of financial doomsday — made my heart pound. Something compelled me to read this article. I picked up the paper and put it into my cart. I knew I was being irrational, but I left the grocery store, tabloid stuffed in my bag, unable to shake the notion that we were about to lose everything.

Hazen returned late Sunday night. I turned up on his doorstep first thing Monday morning.

"I know what you're going to say," I said to him as I held my tabloid in front of his face.

"What's that, Meredith?" he said, showing me into the house.

"Avoid the noise," I answered.

"Yes," he replied slowly. We took our seats in his office. "And no," he continued, a Cheshire cat grin spreading across his face. "The media loves a story — the more terrifying, the better. The pack of journalists was in a honeymoon period with the markets early in the year — stocks could do no wrong. Now, the media is in a feeding frenzy over the 'Coming Great Depression — Markets Crashing,'" he said, gesturing at my tabloid. "That's noise. Yes, stocks do not only go up in value, but we're not about to enter the Dirty Thirties again, either. That's the noise we should all avoid. But this is noise of a different sort, and I think we should listen to it for lessons about investing in the markets for the long term. In fact, I'm glad this market turmoil is occurring now. That means I can address these issues in my seminar."

"Will these lessons alleviate some of the anxiety I'm feeling about having a significant portion of my life savings invested in the stock market?" I asked.

"I believe it will," he replied calmly. "The biggest lesson

investors need to learn is that markets go down as well as up. We've been riding this bull market since the early 1990s. Nominal returns — that means returns before making an adjustment for inflation — on the TSE 300 for the past three years have ranged from over 14 percent to 28 percent. Real returns — taking inflation into consideration — drop those returns to the 13 to 26 percent range. That's a bit out of whack with the long-term returns the TSE has produced. Over the past 40 years, we've seen nominal returns of 10 percent, real returns of slightly over 5 percent.

"Here's the issue: many of today's investors got into the market during the bull run of the past few years. Just look at the mutual fund numbers — that industry has grown tenfold during the 1990s. There are a lot of new investors — many of them baby boomers who are preparing the groundwork for their retirements. It's very easy to get used to 20 percent returns on your money. Too easy, in fact. Sometimes those easy returns cloud people's judgment and they start to think that if they invested in something a little more exotic, they could reap a 30 percent return. They don't have the experience with the downs and ups of the market to understand that 'exotic' is a euphemism for risky. When you think the markets can only go up, it's easy to gloss over risk and find yourself invested in things that are not solid, blue-chip investments. Reviewing the markets over the past century, we see declines of 25 percent or more about once every six years. These big declines are a normal part of the way markets work. It is important to note, however, that markets tend to rise more often than they fall. Let's look at the U.S. stock market. It has risen about three-quarters of the time over the past 50 years. And when it does decline, those periods seldom last more than a year."

"You're making me nervous just talking about risk," I interjected.

"We tend to perceive risk in funny ways," Hazen said. "Consider the TSE. Over the past 15 years, it has returned approximately 12 percent annually. But, the investor must realize that 12 percent is just an average. To get that 12 percent for 15 years, the investor had to endure a roller-coaster ride of plunges of over 20 percent in the value of the market. That happened back on Black Monday, October 19, 1987. Studies have shown that people tend to identify situations where large-scale consequences occur as the riskiest of all. That means that people think flying is riskier than driving a car. When a plane goes down hundreds of people die in one fell swoop. They ignore the fact, however, that tens of thousands more Canadians will die in car accidents in a year than will perish in plane crashes. In the same way, people look at corrections in the stock markets and say: 'This is too risky for me. I've got to get out now!' They shouldn't feel that way if they truly understand the real risks of the market. These big drops are a natural part of the way the markets work. Investors need to know that what goes down does come up — *and vice versa.*"

"So," I said. "This time it's *not* different. Is that what you're saying?"

"Precisely," he replied. "But there are plenty of things that *are* different about these markets today."

"What's so new?"

"The global marketplace, for starters," began Hazen. "Commentators are calling it a 'one-economy world.' The U.S. Federal Reserve chairman said recently that the U.S. — and Canada's economy is tightly tied to that south of the border — cannot remain an 'oasis of prosperity' in a world that is experiencing financial stress. No longer is the U.S. — and, by extension, Canada — living in economic isolation."

"But what does this global marketplace mean for North American investors?" I asked.

"In the long run, it means new opportunities. During the era of communism, many economies were closed to outside investors. With the world opening up, it means new markets for North American companies to grow into. The short run, as we're seeing now, is a different story. I predict that 'emerging markets' will become dirty words for the next year or so until some of the problems we're seeing get worked out. Many experts are questioning whether an unfettered flow of capital from the developed countries to emerging markets is good or bad. Money that comes in quickly to those developing countries can leave equally quickly, devastating a budding economy. And, yes, turmoil in the global markets will affect certain sectors of the North American economy — we've seen the commodity and resource sectors take quite a hit courtesy of these troubles. But don't overstate the problem, either. The Russian economy is going through a very tumultuous period. I feel sorry for those living in Russia today; they're in for a tough time. But, Meredith, Russia accounts for less than 1 percent of the exports of both Canada and the U.S. We've got to keep things in perspective."

"Okay, you're telling me that we're going global and that's a good thing, but there are a few bugs that need to get worked out as we grope towards the future," I stated.

"You've got it," Hazen said, smiling. "But there are other differences we need to examine as well. Let me give you my short list of those differences that I'll work through with you: plummeting interest and inflation rates, a different bear and educated boomers. I'll begin with the interest and inflation rates. As you know, it takes two to tango, and the levels of inflation and interest rates dance together. If inflation is rising, so are interest rates, and vice versa. Whichever way inflation and interest rates go, stock markets move in the opposite direction. What are we seeing today? Inflation is way down from its heyday in the 1970s and early '80s. Interest rates are falling, and I predict they will continue to fall. This means there's plenty of room for the stock markets to move upward. That's a very different environment for many boomers — they're used to the bad old days of high inflation and soaring interest rates. Plus, all the fearmongering about the possibility of a recession needs to be thoroughly examined. Recessions are typically the result of *rising* interest rates used to dampen an inflationary economy. We don't have that situation today. Instead, we have companies operating profitably in a low-inflation, low-interest-rate environment. This is the recipe for a healthy economy and strong stock markets. Our fundamentals are solid."

"Okay, that's a good omen for markets. But I want to know what's different about this bear," I said.

"Some economists are characterizing this bear as a short-term blip in a long-term bull market. Why? Well, many are looking at boomers like you, Meredith, as the cornerstone of that long-term bull — *educated* boomers preparing for their retirements."

"What difference does our level of education make?" I countered.

"Knowing how the markets function will ensure that a turbulent period will not knock you out of your equity investments. Look ahead. We're in for some volatility in the markets courtesy of the millennium bug. But the markets will cope with it. Y2K will probably be like a 24-hour flu, an inconvenience, but not long lasting. And many boomers know that while 20 percent returns are a wondrous sight to behold, this is not the historical norm for the stock market," he said.

"It's one thing to understand that but quite another to see your investments evaporate as the markets tumble," I replied.

"That's a fair comment. Even though you might be anxious, if you have a long-term investment plan in place — and many educated boomers do now — you know that you should sit tight and not sell off your holdings. I predict that, courtesy of the educated boomers, we will not see a stampede out of mutual funds and stocks. We may see boomers refrain from putting additional funds into the market until the current turmoil settles. That's natural. I don't recommend altering your long-term investment strategy even if the seas do get choppy, however. I'm a firm believer in dollar-cost averaging, investing a certain amount of money at regular intervals, no matter where the market is headed. Here's the thing — the market could be up 20 percent or down 20 percent, my message simply does not change. In fact, when the market goes down, your dollar goes further. Even though you will probably experience losses along the way, dollar-cost averaging does tend to lower the average cost of the stocks you buy for your investment portfolio."

"I think I agree with you," I commented. "But for different reasons. From our perspective, we need to invest our savings somewhere. Right now, there's not much else out there but the stock market."

"Well," said Hazen, "that's a good approach for you and Pieter. You're still a long way off from retirement — you don't need your money for many years. But those who are only a couple of years from relying on their funds — let's say they're sending a daughter to university next year or planning a major renovation to their home within a year or two — should look long and hard at ensuring that a portion of their portfolio is invested in bonds, GICs, or money market funds. These people should be seriously talking with their financial advisers about asset diversification strategies. Not everybody is as fortunate as my friend Frank Wallace, who has a healthy pension and for whom a stock portfolio provides *extra* funds. Also, those who really cannot stomach the volatility of the market should think about other investment strategies. You have to be able to endure short-term volatility — that's the 'equity risk premium' stockholders pay — to get the long-term benefits of the market."

"I must admit that I have my moments of doubting the markets. And that's part of the reason Pieter and I also invest in bonds and money market funds, but I understand the math." I chuckled. "I know that the stock market is my best long-run investment. And, right now, Pieter and I have plenty of time."

"Interesting you should say that," replied Hazen. "'Change is the law of life. And those who look only to the past or the present are certain to miss the future.'"

"That sounds pretty profound."

"John Kennedy said that. I believe it's an apt quotation for this discussion. We are seeing changes in the markets. We just talked about a few of them. As Kennedy knew, change is an integral part of our lives. Understanding that dynamic forces us to look to the future. And that's where demographics comes in. You said that you and Pieter still have many years to prepare for your retirement. You and millions of other boomers across North America. Demographics gives us a very powerful tool to look into our future."

I picked up the tabloid with its inflammatory headlines, folded it and stuffed it into Hazen's wastebasket.

I was certainly glad I had my "stock therapy" session with Hazen because the market got worse before it got better. Three days later, on Thursday, August 27, the market took another nasty tumble. The TSE fell more than 370 points to close at 5799.50, a drop of more than 6 percent — in *one* day! I knew that wasn't nearly as bad as Black Monday in 1987, but *I* didn't have my own money in the markets back then. I knew the right approach was to sit tight. Pieter and I did just that.

Our friends Rick and Margo had invited us to join them for dinner on Saturday night. We'd become fast friends with Rick and Margo over the past 10 years. Our sons had brought us together — Malcolm and Andrew had met way back on the very first day of junior kindergarten, and although now attending different schools, they remained best friends. "Frugal" is the best word I can use to describe Rick and Margo. Generous to a fault, our friends are definitely not cheap or penny-pinching, but they certainly know how to save. Neither have big-income jobs; Rick is a social worker and Margo teaches school. Younger than Pieter and I, they had their home — a modest house in the Civic Hospital neighbourhood near the Glebe — paid off within five years of buying the place. Investing is Rick's hobby. A voracious reader, he devours the financial pages of the *Globe* and the *Citizen*, plus he reads *Fortune*, *Investor's Digest* and the like religiously. Now, Margo tells me, he spends an hour or two nearly every evening cruising his favourite web sites for financial information.

The kids were both at sleepovers. Malcolm was actually already at Rick and Margo's place, hanging out with Andrew. Pieter suggested we walk to dinner. "It'll only take us about 45 minutes," he said. "If we stay late, I'm sure that Rick or Margo will give us a lift back."

"Good idea," I replied, fetching a light sweater. "It's a gorgeous evening. Plus, we'll save some gas."

"Boy," said Pieter, "you're quite the tightwad tonight."

"Spending time with Rick and Margo always makes me think about how much money we throw away. They're both so good about money," I explained. As we walked to the sidewalk, I noticed Hazen and Ruth leaving Hazen's place.

"Hello," I shouted, waving to them. They crossed the street, ready to chat.

"We're off for a stroll by the canal," said Ruth. "Isn't it a perfect summer evening?"

"We're about to embarrass our son," Hazen said with a chuckle. "After our walk, we're going to drop by that new diner on Bank for our dinner. Dylan's working there tonight, you know."

"Does he know you're coming?" asked Pieter.

"Oh, no," replied Ruth. "If we'd told him our plans, he would have flipped. Nope — we're going to surprise him."

"I'm sure he'll love that," I said.

"Oh, I plan on leaving him a nice big tip to ease the blow of having to serve his parents," joked Hazen. "Well, we'd better be off."

Ruth slipped her hand into the crook of Hazen's arm, and as Pieter and I headed in the opposite direction, I slipped my hand into the crook of Pieter's arm. It felt very cozy and comfortable.

In any conversation with Rick it was only a matter of time before the talk turned to investing, the markets, the economy. By the time dessert was served, we'd already covered the turmoil in the global marketplace and the impact that it would have on North American markets and we were well into a discussion of investor psychology and the media's attempts to build the current stock market woes into a crisis of enormous proportions.

"I read an interview with Robert Rubin in *Fortune* the other day," said Rick as he brought a bowl of fruit salad to the table. "He's the U.S. treasury secretary. He reminded readers of a very important fact. 'Economies are built on confidence,' he said. If that confidence falters — whether or not there are valid reasons for the slip — the economy suffers. In the same interview, he also had this advice for investors: 'In a strong environment don't get caught up in the euphoria. In a bad environment, don't get caught up in the concerns.' I'm not going to allow the prophets of doom who want a hot story to alter my investing strategy, which is simple: invest regularly and patiently."

I said, "Over the past few years, we've seen plenty of investors 'caught in the euphoria,' thinking the market only went one way — up."

"That's one reason this market instability is very, very good," stated Rick emphatically. "This market downturn is teaching novice investors a lesson that they need to know."

"That's one of Hazen's themes too," I added.

"Plus," Rick continued, "learning that a market can go down as well as up will also teach investors that they need to save in order to increase their wealth. I think that many new investors were caught up in the euphoric 'wealth effect,' spending because the value of their assets, courtesy of the stock markets, was increasing at such an incredible clip. Too many wanted to believe that they could appreciate their way to affluence. Yes, assets do appreciate over time, but not at the rate that some of these folks began to think. Then factor in declining interest rates — that made servicing debts, like repaying mortgages, cheaper. That also made a lot of people feel a lot richer. In fact, the savings rate turned negative recently as withdrawals from savings exceeded new savings. But now, Canadians are back to feeling a bit poorer, courtesy of this turmoil. I'd argue that they needed to be reminded that a solid retirement plan is based, first and foremost, on a savings plan."

"You're harsh in your opinions," interjected Pieter. "Talking about saving is a much easier task than actually socking away the money."

"Life is all about choices," said Margo. "In this materialistic world of ours, it's not easy to say no. But that's what saving is all about. I really don't think Rick and I are cheapskates, but we try to be thoughtful about where our pennies are going. Eating at home instead of ordering in from the pizza place around the corner. Saving up until you have the cash — not using that all-too-easy credit card — to buy a new winter coat or to put a new countertop in the kitchen. Tackling — and reducing — debt. Hey, didn't you two walk here this evening?"

Pieter and I nodded.

"I know it sounds petty," Margo said, "but even little things like walking to appointments, going to the library to borrow a book rather than buying it, reusing wrapping paper, it all adds up — at least, it certainly has added up for us over the years. In the same way that we invest, we're committed to saving — regularly and patiently."

"We've also avoided the real estate trap," added Rick. "We could buy a bigger, flashier house than this," he said, sweeping his hand around their small dining room. "But we would never reap an adequate financial reward from that investment. We can do smarter things with our money. Instead, we'll stay in this small house, which happens to be located in a central and very stable neighbourhood. There will always be a market for a place like this. I don't think the same thing can be said – with the same certainty – about one of those opulent monster houses way out in Dunrobin. It's all about becoming more resourceful. Employers talk about the 'flexible' workplace. To me, that's a euphemism for less job security for employees. My dad had one job and one employer for his entire working career. I bet you can't name one of our contemporaries who can boast a regular, lifelong paycheque like that. It comes as no surprise that we're seeing the gap between the haves and have-nots widening in our society. For all these reasons, many people are feeling economically exposed and insecure. We're on our own. I think that growing realization will make many people become more like us in the long term – resourceful, frugal savers."

As Rick finished his mini-lecture on the state of the world, we heard the boys come in the back door. They were returning from a movie and came into the dining room to see if they could score some leftover dessert. Margo found a couple of extra bowls, dished out some fruit salad and passed them a tray of brownies.

"We went to the place that only charges two dollars for a movie," said Malcolm. "I still have money left over."

"Save it!" commanded Pieter, a smile spreading across his face. The adults laughed.

The boys shared that complicit smile of teen-age conspirators. Translation: "Aren't our parents geeks?"

15

This Time… It's Different

By mid-September, I had finished my work with Hazen. With the research we had assembled over the summer, he started preparing his seminar in earnest. The kids and I headed back to school. I'd always wanted to study child psychology and so, on a whim, I enrolled in a class at the University of Ottawa. I didn't have another contract lined up — although I was sending out resumés like crazy — so I decided I'd keep myself busy with school work until something materialized.

In mid-October, Hazen stopped by the house one afternoon.

"Two things I need to discuss with you, Meredith," he began as I welcomed him in. "First, I was over visiting with Frank and Jean yesterday. They've found a small apartment in a retirement residence out on Carling Avenue.

As a result, they're ready to sell the house. I mentioned that you and Pieter might be interested. They're prepared to entertain a private offer before they list the house with an agent."

"That's interesting news," I replied. "Pieter and I are definitely interested. We'll give them a call. What's your second newsflash?"

"I'm hoping that you'll accompany me to Winnipeg during the first week of November. That's where I'm delivering the new seminar for the first time. I thought you might want to see the results of your summer's handiwork. I'll foot the bill, of course."

"That's a generous offer, Hazen," I replied. "I need to look at my calendar and talk to Pieter to see what he's got going during that time. But, off the top of my head, I think I can swing it. I'd love to go."

October passed in a whirl of school work, Hallowe'en preparations and discussions about our new house. We arrived at a deal with Frank and Jean. They were emotional about leaving the house but delighted to sell it to a family that they knew would tend to it as carefully as they had over the years. We'd spent many hours discussing our offer on the house with Hazen. Like many Canadians, we had finally figured out that a house is a home, not an investment. Hazen showed us a study outlining the reasons why Canadians buy a home: 94 percent wish to be "master of their own domain," while only 49 percent buy for financial security. It was a tough lesson but it served to keep us within our means —

buying a house we could afford now with no illusions that its price would run up dramatically during the time we owned it. We ended up paying $210,000. Reasonable for a street where many of the homes would go for upwards of $300,000 and taking into consideration the amount of work that our home would need to bring it into the next century. Fortunately, Pieter was keen to do much of that work, keeping our renovation costs to a minimum.

Before I knew it, I was seated on a plane next to Hazen, talking about what lay ahead of us in Winnipeg.

A taxi dropped us at the door of the Crowne Plaza Hotel. We found the conference room reserved by the financial institution that Hazen was speaking for. The room was serenely empty, chairs in neat rows with packets of information sitting on each seat. I picked up a folder and peeked in — a brochure for the financial institution, a couple of newspaper clippings about Hazen, copies of the slides that Hazen would be showing during his presentation and a reading list. I recognized that. Hazen and I had worked on it over the summer. Hazen insisted it be included, an integral part, he maintained, of the message he wished to deliver to his audiences. If you haven't yet begun, start your financial education now. If you've made a foray into the world of financial publications, keep going back! (Hazen's reading list is reproduced in the back of this book for your information.)

I watched Hazen prepare himself mentally as the hour of the presentation drew closer. The members of the financial institution arrived, greeting him warmly. Slowly, the room filled. Then, it was time.

After a quick introduction by a local manager of the

financial institution (Ruth was right — the introducer did have a bit of fun with Hazen's seminar title, "This Time It's Different"), Hazen strode to the podium. He looked down at the floor for a couple of seconds, then raised his head slowly, passed a penetrating gaze around the audience, and then began to speak.

"This time it will be different. There are many who will tell you that if an investment adviser says this to you, the best thing you can do is to run from the room. In fact, that was the implication contained in the introduction to this seminar. Well, I'd advise you to sit tight and listen to what I have to say over the next 40 minutes or so because this time it is different. Globalization, technology and an aging population. Yes, this time things are really different. You've never seen a Canada like this before," said Hazen, raising his voice. Then he changed gears completely, speaking in a quiet, even tone.

"I'm a believer in education. I believe that investors should spend time educating themselves about the markets they invest in. And I believe that one of the most important things that people need to learn is this simple fact: change happens. We cannot stop change. Change makes things different. To successfully cope with change, we need to know it, understand it and, finally, accept it. In other words, the world moves forward. It's up to you to keep moving with it. Or, and this I guarantee, you will be left behind."

He flipped up a quote on the screen behind him. It read, "In a time of drastic change, it is the learners who inherit the future. The learned usually find themselves equipped to live in a world that no longer exists." He waited a moment, allowing the audience to digest these words. Then he told them that the American essayist Eric Hoffer had written them in 1973. He went on to run through a quick checklist of the changes that have occurred in the world during our lifetimes, highlighting the technological tsunami that has hit all of our lives, the juggernaut of globalization that has transformed our markets, the ongoing march of women into the workforce.

Hazen then moved to his favourite subject, demographics. He highlighted a couple of profound changes in population statistics. Then he pointed out, among other things, the fall in the infant mortality rates in Canada (a decrease of 55 percent from 1975 to 1995) and the rise in life expectancy (in the 1920s, life expectancy at birth was less than 60 for men and slightly over 60 for women; now those numbers have increased to well over 70 for men and 80-plus for women).

"But the change that particularly interests me began back in 1947," he continued. "In fact, I see this change before me. You're the 'extras.' You're the third child — or maybe you're the fourth or fifth in your family. I see you squirming out there. Yes, you know who you are. You're the extra three and one-half million that form the baby boom — over nine and a half million in Canada. From Confederation onwards, the fertility rate in Canada — that's the average number of children born to each woman — fell. It plummeted during the dark days of the Depression. But that long-term trend changed dramatically at the end of the 1940s and continued well into the 1960s. You extras are the result! After hitting a peak of four children per woman in 1959, the fertility rate has now moved back down to less than two children per woman. That means that we live in an aging society. Yes, not only are you extras, but you're also aging extras!" The audience responded with a round of warm laughter.

"The boomers are what I refer to as the pig in the python of Canadian society. You extras, together with your elder brothers and sisters, have been a powerful engine of change since your arrival. No surprise, you account for nearly one-third of the Canadian population. Now you're closing in on middle age, and the Canada you have been used to is going to be very different from here on in. Let's take a quick look at the environment in which you find yourselves. Jobs, for example." Hazen looked out into the audience. "Our jobs are very different from those of our parents. One in four organizations now categorize themselves as 'flexible.' People come and go as needed at these project-oriented companies. This is not employment for life. Companies put a positive spin on this trend, saying it is empowering for workers. It really means: 'You're on your own, pal.' We're seeing changes in the pension plans of many corporations. There has been a significant shift from defined-benefit to defined-contribution plans. Again, corporate Canada is shifting the responsibility to individuals to look out for — to manage — their own future, their own security in retirement. This is different." He paused and cleared his throat gently.

"Further, I believe the way boomers will prepare for their retirements is different from previous generations. You've all heard of the nursery rhyme 'This Little Pig Goes to Market.' Well, I contend that this pig — that's all the boomers in Canada — are going to market — the financial markets, to stock up for their retirement years. Yes, I know that there are those out there who will argue that the pig will get slaughtered in the markets. And there are times when the boomers will feel that way. Let's look at the statistics. Over the past 20 years, the TSE 300 lost at least 15 percent of its value more than six times. That can feel pretty bad when it's your retirement fund you're watching bob up and down in value. But let's take a look at the long haul. Many of you in the audience were born in the mid-1950s. Let's say you had a very wise grandmother who invested $100 in the TSE 300 on the day you were born. And let's say you kept that money invested and reinvested the dividends. Today, you'd be sitting on an investment worth nearly $5,000. If your granny had invested in bonds, that number would be about $3,000. If she'd chosen treasury bills, you'd have about $2,000. Aren't you glad she chose stocks? The pig, when it hits financial markets over the next two decades, is going to make a big difference to the market as we know it today. Remember, not only are you boomers going to be investing individually but you'll also be bringing your mighty muscle to mutual funds and pension funds. We can already see the power of large pension funds in Canada. Look at the Ontario Teachers Pension Plan — over $50 billion in assets. Much of that money is earmarked for boomers and, in the meantime, much of it is headed to financial markets. This is different."

Again he looked to the floor, then raised his head slowly. "But some things never change. You've all heard the expression *plus ça change, plus c'est la même chose.* The more things change, the more they remain the same. Human nature doesn't change very much, for example. Greed and fear have been with us since our very beginnings. 'Greed and fear might be human,' says Montreal-based money manager Stephen Jarislowsky, 'but they are not traits of a good investor.' He's absolutely right. We've seen the workings of greed and fear in our marketplace during the 1990s – investors became seduced by 20 percent returns on their stock portfolios and wanted more. When the market ran into trouble this past August, we saw many of those investors dump their equity holdings out of fear. Maybe many of you wanted out of the markets at that time."

I looked around the audience; many heads were nodding in agreement.

"The traits of a good investor are knowledge and patience – an understanding of the long-term workings of the market and the ability to weather the storms that the market is destined to endure. When this pig goes to market, it should demonstrate that pigs are the smartest animals in the barnyard and learn that greed will not pay." I listened as Hazen presented his Lions, Tigers and Bears theory to the audience.

"Another thing that's fundamental human nature – we seem to like bad news," continued Hazen. "We squirmed in August and September as the markets roiled. Then, the subject of the markets seemed to fall from view in October. Well, this past October saw the best performance in North American markets in more than 15 years, as they staged a month-long rally. Nobody likes good news, I guess." Hazen lifted his hands as a soft chuckle rolled through the audience.

"And the market turmoil did yield up its fair share of good news. According to the Investment Funds Institute of Canada, assets in funds managed by its members dropped more than $30 billion in value between June 30 and September 30 of this year. Mutual fund sales dropped dramatically in September. But — here's the good news — there was no real increase in redemptions. In other words, investors held fast to the funds already in their portfolios. 'There's no rush for the exits,' commented Dan Richards of the consulting firm Marketing Solutions. People are learning that there will be ups and downs in the market." He stopped and walked across the stage.

"Successful investors will learn to find a path through the changes occurring as we speak while recognizing the permanence of other things." He paused again. "Like the fundamentals that rule the marketplace. Equity prices reflect the earnings of the companies that issue those stocks. That's basic. Interest rates will always affect stock prices. The rule? When interest rates are low, stock prices rise. High interest rates, on the other hand, depress the value of stocks." Hazen then provided a thumbnail outline of his views on current valuations and the future trend of interest rates (down courtesy of the boomers).

"Earnings and interest rates," he concluded."They're the foundation — the Canadian Shield of the marketplace, if you will. But what we build on that foundation changes over time. Let me give you two examples. Let's look at a Canadian food retailer that I think understands the demographic reality of this country — Loblaws. This company recently announced a takeover bid for Quebec food retailer Provigo. This bid is all about the consolidation that's currently occurring in the food industry as retailers prepare to do battle with a foreign behemoth. Put your ear to the ground. You can hear Wal-Mart galloping into town. But what was of great interest to me was the actual announcement of the merger between Loblaws and Provigo. According to a Loblaws vice-president, this is 'a good transaction for our shareholders.' Sounds simple, right? But the stated goal of maximizing shareholder value is one of the items that we build on the foundation of earnings and interest rates. A company's commitment to shareholder value is one of the things that increases the value of a stock. Loblaws' announcement reflects a solid recognition shared by many North American companies: shareholders and the prices of the shares they hold are critical. That recognition itself has served to increase the value of those shares." He stopped for a moment and walked across the stage again.

"Now, here's my other example. We all know that boomers can consume — everything from cars to furniture to soup to nuts. Well, it's that consumption that drives the earnings of many companies. And healthy earnings translate into healthy stock prices. For more examples, take a look at Harry Dent's book, *The Roaring 2000s*."

I looked around the audience. People were definitely interested in Hazen's message.

"So, where does all of this leave you, the investor?" I could see that Hazen was changing gears. He'd sketched in the big picture for the audience — a world filled with constant change, the need to keep up with those changes, a nod to the fundamentals that don't change. I figured that he would now hit on his favourite topic, the impact of the boomers on financial markets. When I heard his next sentence, I knew that I had figured right.

"The newspapers are filled with scare stories about the boomers' inability to save, their unpreparedness for retirement. There is some truth to the savings story. The savings rate in this country is at historic lows. Here's a newsflash: look at the demographics. The boomers are at a point in their lives where saving is a Herculean task, what with kids and mortgages. It's the timing, folks. You just wait." Hazen summarized the various savings theories, concluding that the era of savings was fast approaching as boomers paid off their mortgages and waved goodbye to the kids. I was delighted to see my work in action.

"A critical component of the savings decision is education," continued Hazen. "And I hope that boomers are listening to the message: save if you want a comfortable retirement. Save early, patiently and regularly." He recited the last words firmly and evenly. There was no mistaking his message.

"Now, saving is not an easy task." Hazen had changed his tone slightly. He was less emphatic, more encouraging. "And that's where our low interest rates will help us. Plus, our governments are starting to practice fiscal responsibility. That's something I am happy to include in my theme of 'this time it's different.'" People smiled at that comment.

"This will be a good thing for many Canadians. First, declining interest rates will mean lower mortgage payments. And that means more money in the pockets of Canadians. As governments begin balancing their books, that means that the supply of new debt is shrinking. Think about it. Governments raised all that money they used to spend by issuing bonds. Bonds are a financial commodity like anything else, and the boomers, with savings to invest, are headed directly at them. If, however, the demand is increasing while the supply is shrinking, we know what will happen. People will be willing to pay more for them — the law of supply and demand. And that, my friends, will keep interest rates low — there's an inverse relationship between the value of bonds and interest rates. Now, here's what's different. Interest rates used to set the trend. Now bonds — or, more precisely, the dearth of bonds — will determine what rates will be. The tail is wagging the dog."

I wondered when he was going to bring his boomers back into the discussion. I didn't need to wait long.

"Boomers are the other factor that will keep interest rates low. As I mentioned earlier, Canada is headed to a time where there will be dramatically more savers then spenders, as the boomers age and begin preparing for retirement. Because of this preponderance of savers, your money just won't get much of a return because everybody will be doing it — saving, that is. In fact, I think you might walk into a bank with your savings in hand and they'll charge you for keeping your money. You'll be a nuisance to them!" The audience roared at that one. Next, he outlined his views on real estate. The tone of the audience was a bit more serious now as they learned that many of them have far too much money wrapped up in this asset.

Now it was time for his finale. He waded headlong into the subject of the stock market.

"I'd like to talk to you now about the markets, a commodity that is very different this time around. Until now, the boomers haven't been saving all that much but they certainly have been turning their attention to the markets. To date, their vehicle of choice has been the mutual fund. As the boomers age, we've seen a dramatic shift in the way Canadians invest. According to the Investment Funds Institute of Canada, the growth rate of the industry is accelerating — it took 60 years for the Canadian mutual fund industry to reach $100 billion, four and a half years to hit the next $200 billion, and only 18 months to reach $300 billion. And Canadians are filling their RRSPs with mutual funds. Mutual funds account for nearly half of the portfolio value of those RRSPs. Now it's a matter of wait and see — what will happen when the boomers really put their energies into accumulating their retirement nest eggs?"

Hazen fleshed out his theories on the boomers' future investment strategies and the pressure they were bound to place on the financial markets. Then he turned to reassuring the nervous types in the audience — like me.

"Let me begin by telling you that nobody really knows for certain where markets are headed. But, part of intelligent investing involves making educated guesses. And in any educated investor's arsenal you will find demographic information. But applying that demographic information can lead to unsettling questions. The two that I'm most often asked to address are these: If the market is flooded by boomers, doesn't that destabilize the marketplace? And what happens to the golden era of the stock market when all those boomers retire and cash out?" He paused for a moment.

"Good questions. And no one knows — with certainty — the answers to these questions. I will, however, provide you with my opinion. I believe that the average Joe will prove to be a stabilizing effect on the marketplace, rewriting the old adage that when the common man invests in the market it's time for the experts to bail. I think most folks today realize that they're in the market for the long term — that's at least 20 years. They know that the markets have their ups and downs. They're learning how to handle those times of turmoil. A lot of people thought they knew what their risk tolerance was, but it wasn't until this past August that they got the opportunity to really test that tolerance." Hazen smiled wryly, watching many in the audience nod in agreement.

"If the market turmoil in August is any example, it's the average guy who's in for the long haul. As I mentioned earlier, the statistics show that individual investors held firm. Now for the second question. What's going to happen when the boomers need all that money they have invested in the stock market, when they retire and cash out? Will it be market meltdown time? I don't believe it will. First, let's get things into perspective. The peak of the baby boomers' retirement years does not occur until the 2030s. Now, I like to talk about the long term, but that's over 30 years away. Lots of things we can't anticipate can happen in that time. Just look at the *last* 30 years — things like computers, the Internet and Velcro have changed our lives." I laughed out loud at Hazen's Velcro reference.

"Now, let's not cut our noses off to spite our faces. Don't miss out on the next couple of decades in the marketplace because we're worried about something 30 years out. Now's the time to build that comfortable cushion of wealth to take you through your retirement years. Okay, now to answer the question. There's no doubt that there probably will be a significant risk of a long-lasting bear market. But there are a few things to keep in mind. First, all boomers are not going to wake up one morning and decide to cash out of the markets on the same day. The process will be gradual and take many years to unwind. What we've got to keep in mind is that, as the world has transformed itself into a global marketplace, North American stocks, issued by companies like Loblaws that pay careful attention to their shareholders, are of great interest to investors from around the globe. These may be the investors who line up to buy the boomers' stocks. But that, my friends, is pure speculation about a time that I will probably not be around to see. All I can say is have fun." Hazen walked to his computer and flipped up a slide showing a list of companies. I recognized it immediately — it was my fad-versus-trend list.

"We've talked about the pull that boomers will exert on the stock markets as they age. The demand that the boomers will place on markets will serve to pull the prices of that commodity up. But the boomers also push the market by pushing the earnings of North American companies. And, as I've already mentioned to you, higher earnings tend to translate into higher stock prices. What do I mean? Look at the companies on this list. They sell things to the boomers. How many of you have been to Disney World? Who's bought eyeglasses recently? As Bill Sterling and Stephen Waite point out in their book, *Boomernomics*, 'it can't hurt to invest with the demographic odds in your favour.'"

Hazen outlined his theories on fad versus trend companies. Then he took the audience on a quick tour of global and domestic demographic trends, highlighting the type of companies poised to benefit from those trends. He discussed his preference for blue-chip stocks issued by large, reputable companies, pointing to the recent TSE experience of large capitalization stocks (stocks with a market capitalization of over $1 billion). So far in 1998, large cap stocks fared much better than smaller cap ones.

"Today, boomers are pushing the earnings of many companies by consuming massive amounts of their products. Plus, they're pulling the valuations of those stocks as they acquire them in their drive to prepare for retirement. It's a double whammy for the markets." He flipped up a final slide.

"I will leave you with a Yiddish aphorism that is a favourite of a dear friend of mine. 'Hope for miracles but don't rely on one,'" he read from his slide. "Now, I'm sure you're wondering how this fits with my theme this evening." I glanced around the room. Sure enough, there were several mystified faces in the audience.

"It certainly would be wonderful to win Lotto 6/49,

but don't make buying lottery tickets your major form of retirement planning. And don't count on double-digit gains in the stock market either. Be honest with yourself and recognize your own shortcomings. Begin by educating yourself on the ways of the market. I've given you a quick overview of one of the tools — demographics — that can provide you with a clear insight into the market. There are many others. Learn about them too. Give serious consideration to obtaining professional advice from a financial planner or stockbroker. Would you think of roofing your house or drilling your own teeth? Enough said. The first step is to determine how much you'll need to save to provide for the retirement you want to enjoy. That's your goal. You don't need miracles to make it happen. Thank you for your kind attention this evening."

As he stepped from the stage, applause rolled through the audience. I watched several people surround Hazen, posing questions, challenging his theories. After about 15 minutes, he made his way over to my seat.

"So? What did you think?" he asked.

"You were great, but I'm not surprised. All of your effort paid off."

"We'll save the surprises for tomorrow, then," he replied mysteriously. "We've been invited to join some people from the financial institution for supper. Are you interested?"

I nodded. Collecting my briefcase and jacket, I wondered what on earth lay in store for me tomorrow.

16

Taking Care of Unfinished Business

We caught the early-morning flight out of Winnipeg the day after Hazen's seminar. As we were taxiing down the runway at six-forty-five, I suddenly remembered Hazen's promised surprise.

"So," I said after we watched Winnipeg fade into the distance, "I haven't seen any surprises so far today."

"The morning is still young," he replied with a smile. "But I guarantee that you'll have your surprise before the morning's out and I promise that you'll be bowled over by this one." At that moment, the flight attendant arrived with our breakfast and I could tell that I would hear no more until Hazen was ready.

We covered a lot of territory during that flight, never once touching on demographics. We talked about our plans for the house. Hazen listened to me talk about my friend Sharon, her cancer treatments, her prognosis. I told him of my plans to visit her during the Christmas vacation — I planned to take the train down to Toronto and meet Sharon there. We'd stay in a hotel and treat ourselves to a night at the theatre and a couple of good meals. Then we'd sightsee and, most important, we'd talk. We mused about the way hardship crystallizes the issues in one's life, bringing into sharp focus the things that really matter — people, specifically family and friends.

Our conversation rambled through reminiscences of times past, some stories side-splittingly funny, others sad, still others frankly sentimental and silly. And then we were home, circling over the Ottawa airport.

As we walked into the airport, I caught sight of Pieter, next to Ruth and Dylan.

"Hazen, look," I said, pointing to their three smiling faces. "I thought we were taking a cab in from the airport."

"The surprise is just beginning to unfold," he replied.

Sure enough, as I got closer to the three of them, I realized they were all gussied up. Pieter was wearing a suit, attire he never wears to the office. Dylan sported a jacket and tie. I didn't even know he owned such fancy duds. Ruth was a vision, splendidly elegant in a tailored suit of cranberry silk. And she had her hair swept up. Could those be real flowers in her coiffure, I wondered as I walked towards them.

I didn't have long to wait for an explanation.

"Did you tell her?" asked Ruth.

Hazen laughed. "No, I kept to my original plan. She knows nothing."

"You two are terrible," said Dylan.

Pieter kissed me, taking my briefcase from my hand. I asked about the kids and he reassured me that they had made it to school this morning and they hadn't even missed me.

"It's not only us," continued Ruth. "Pieter is in on the surprise too!"

"What on earth is going on here?" I asked, a bit miffed at being left out of a secret that everyone but me was in on.

"We're going to a wedding," answered Hazen. "Right now. It starts at eleven. Let's get cracking. We've only got a half-hour to get there."

My mouth dropped and, before I collected my thoughts, Ruth put her arm around my shoulders.

"Meredith, will you stand up for me? I'm getting married this morning."

The rest of the morning passed in a blur. Pieter hustled us into our van and we headed to the courthouse on Elgin Street. There, in a stark, government-issue chapel, a justice of the peace performed a quick ceremony. Ruth had come prepared with simple bouquets of white lilies for both of us. Dylan, who stood up for his father, and Hazen both sported white roses in their lapels. Ruth and Hazen exchanged their vows in a completely businesslike manner with very little emotion. Even when they kissed, it was a tiny little smooch, the kind friends exchange when they meet at a party.

We were back out on the sidewalk by noon. As the office workers hustled by us on their way to lunch,

Hazen announced that he and Ruth had made plans for a special wedding luncheon at his favourite restaurant, a charming spot in the Gatineau Hills, appropriately called Métamorphose — a subtle nod to his theme of change. Once again, Pieter bundled us all into our van and we headed for the hills.

By the time the champagne had been uncorked and a few friends had joined the party, we finally had the chance to sit and everyone had started to relax. Hazen's arm was draped around Ruth. Dylan was sitting at the head of the table, beaming with happiness. Pieter, I could tell, was still enjoying my enormous shock at the entire affair.

"But, but, but I didn't even know you two were considering this," I began.

"Well, we don't tell you everything," answered Ruth with a smile. Surprise is the greatest gift which life can give us. We thought you'd enjoy this surprising gift of a wedding. That's why we held tight to our secret. Meredith, you, together with Dylan, served as the catalysts that brought us together this summer. And the two of you made us realize that our time had come. Do you remember when you suggested that we should work on a book together?"

I nodded.

Hazen said, "We took that suggestion more seriously than you thought. We began meeting to talk about the concept; regular meetings, several times each week. Then Dylan arrived back home and our meetings took on a more sociable air." He looked at Ruth, then suddenly leaned towards her and gave her the long, romantic kiss that their wedding ceremony had lacked. As they parted, I noticed that Ruth was crying.

"Mom," said Dylan, "what's the matter?"

"I know you're all going to groan," she said, dabbing her eyes with the edge of her napkin. "My uncle Jack always said, 'When the heart is full, the eyes overflow.' I'm just happy. Simple as that."

"Happiness," said Hazen quietly. "I'd like to begin my married life with a toast to happiness."

We raised our glasses and drank deeply of the champagne.

Ruth said, "Hazen's not telling you the entire story, Meredith. We started talking about the possibility of marriage seriously when we were discussing a study by a professor at Oxford on the subject of happiness. His conclusion? The key to happiness is having one close relationship and a network of friends. We looked at each other and realized that we were one another's one close relationship. And we had been for decades. So, why didn't we just get on with it and get married?"

"But marriage seems far too conventional for the two of you," I answered.

"We spend so much of our lives caught — trapped, really — in our immediate concerns," Hazen responded. "Is dinner ready? Do I have clean socks? Where are my car keys? We miss the big picture. We overlook the big questions. Why am I here? Who really matters to me? What will happen when I am gone? I guess it's natural to begin thinking more about the big issues as we age. The realization of mortality tends to clear the mind and, with the kids out of the house, we have more time to ponder the imponderables." He chuckled, pointing down the table at Dylan. "To answer your challenge, the time was right. We had both moved into a different phase of our lives."

"So," I said slowly, staring across the table at one of my favourite married couples. "Are you telling me that 'this time it's different'?"

"*Vive la différence*," responded Hazen, lifting his glass once more.

Useful Resources

Books

Adams, Michael. *Sex in the Snow: Canadian Social Values at the End of the Millennium*. Toronto: Viking, 1997.

Chand, Ranga. *Chand's World of Mutual Funds*. Toronto: Stoddart, 1999.

Chilton, David. *The Wealthy Barber: The Common Sense Guide to Successful Financial Planning*. Toronto: Stoddart, 1989.

Chevreau, Jonathan with Ellis, Michael and Rogers, S. Kelly. *The Wealthy Boomer:* Life After Mutual Funds. Toronto: Key Porter, 1998.

Cohen, Bruce with Diamond, Alyssa. *The Money Adviser: The Canadian Guide to Successful Financial Planning*, second revised paperback edition. Toronto: Stoddart, 1999.

Dent, Harry S., Jr. *The Roaring 2000s: Building the Wealth and Lifestyle You Desire in the Greatest Boom in History*. New York: Simon & Schuster, 1998.

Dychtwald, Ken and Flower, Joe. *Age Wave: How the Most Important Trend of Our Time Will Change Your Future.* New York: Bantam Doubleday Dell, 1990.

Foot, David K. and Stoffman, Daniel. *Boom, Bust & Echo 2000: Profiting from the Demographic Shift in the New Millennium.* Toronto: Macfarlane Walter & Ross, 1998.

Gardiner, Robert M. *The Dean Witter Guide to Personal Investing*, revised edition. New York: Dutton, 1997.

Lynch, Peter with Rothchild, John. *Beating the Street.* New York: Simon & Schuster, 1993.

Martin, Tony. *Me and My Money.* Toronto: Macmillan Canada, 1998.

Moses, Barbara. *Career Intelligence: Mastering the New Work and Personal Realities.* Toronto: Stoddart, 1997.

Reid, Angus. *Shakedown: How the New Economy Is Changing Our Lives.* Toronto: Doubleday Canada, 1996.

Siegel, Jeremy J. *Stocks for the Long Run: The Definitive Guide to Financial Market Returns and Long-Term Investment Strategies*, second edition. New York: McGraw-Hill, 1998.

Sterling, William and Waite, Stephen. *Boomernomics: The Future of Your Money in the Upcoming Generational Warfare.* New York: Library of Contemporary Thought, Ballantine, 1998.

Thurow, Lester C. *The Future of Capitalism: How Today's Economic Forces Shape Tomorrow's World.* New York: Penguin, 1996.

Yamada, Louise. *Market Magic: Riding the Greatest Bull Market of the Century.* New York: John Wiley & Sons, 1998.

Newspapers and Newsletters

Globe and Mail, Report on Business section

Investor's Digest of Canada, 133 Richmond St. W., Toronto, ON, M5H 3M8